L.R.N.D.

A special

"Thank You"

goes out to these

Friends of LRND

who made a

contribution to

the publishing of

this book aiding

in our efforts to

break the cycle of

incarceration.

1. The Autrey & Richardson Families

2. Women of Louisiana Correctional Institute for Women

3. Men of Angola State Penitentiary

4. Stop The Killings, Inc.-Silky Slim

5. Families of Louisiana's Incarcerated

6. The Malone Law Firm

7. Leon Wheeler & Associates

8. Gigi's Entertainment Complex-Shreveport, LA

9. Inner City Entrepreneur Institute-Roy Burrell, Director

10. Higher Ground Ministries-Rev. and Mrs. Morris

11. Major Topics Radio Talk Show-Baton Rouge

12. Southern University- Shreveport, LA

13. Gardner's Carpet Cleaners-Les Gardner

14. The Honorable Richard Z. Johnson, Jr.-District Attorney, DeSoto Parish

15. CityView Realty-Juanita Lester

16. DeSoto Parish Schools

17. Louisiana Clergy

18. Mind, Body, & Soul-Terri Pugh

19. The Gentleman's Closet-Terry Williams

20. The Shreveport Sun

DEDICATION

To all that continued to ask me
when is the book coming…

Here it is!

Lessons LRND from...

THE ONE THAT GOT AWAY

A True Story of Personal Transformation

8/26/10

FOX RICH TELLS ALL

L.R.N.D.
PUBLISHING

Peace Blessing
Velonie
U R Powerful
I don't u forget
This life is what
u make it !
Fox Rich

LRND Publishing books may be purchased at a special discount when ordered in bulk quantities. For more information please visit our website at www.LRND.org

For immediate response email foxrich@foxrich.com

The One That Got Away

Cover Design and Book Layout: Stark Imagery Digital Design

Text Reformating: Eli Blyden | crunchtimeg@msn.com

Editing: Sonya Landry - Editor | Shreveport Sun &

Editing: Kojo Livingston - Editor | Destiny One Jounal

Makeup : Meka Bennett - Celebrety Make-up Artist | My Spa My Way

ISBN : 978-0-578-03819-3

PRINTED IN THE UNITED STATES OF AMERICA

FROM THE DESK OF
The Honorable Richard Z. Johnson, Jr.
District Attorney, DeSoto Parish

To the Students of DeSoto Parish:

Hello and best wishes to each one of you. Over the years, I have gotten to know many of you and your families. It is because of this relationship that I am concerned about each of you and your well being.

As your District Attorney, I have seen the results that bad choices have made in the lives of many of our fellow citizens which has lead me to not only work to prosecute those who cross the line- but also to work to prevent our future leaders from seeing the path of crime as an option. Out of these prevention efforts and my fervent desire to assist you in avoiding bad choices, I present this book as my gift to you with hopes that Fox Rich's story of transformation will divert you from taking the wrong road.

Dream and dream BIG! I know that you have within you the ability, the drive and the determination to be successful in life. I believe that you can do and be anything that you want to do. Within your ranks may be the next district attorney, judge, sheriff, congressman or congresswoman, governor or even President. With your ranks are future doctors, lawyers, entrepreneurs and teachers.

But success does not come without trials and tribulations. Success comes to those who persevere through the struggles that life has to offer. Success does not mean that you never failed. It only means that you did not let the failures discourage you and that you fought through the hardships until you obtained your goal.

This book is about one woman who struggled through the trials and tribulations of life. It is about a woman who had the fortitude to not let one misstep in her life prevent her from obtaining the blessings that God had in store for her. It is about a woman who serves as an inspiration to us all and shows us that we can overcome our mistakes and still achieve our dreams.

Read this book and learn from it.

I give you my love and wish you the best that life has to offer!

The Honorable Richard Z. Johnson, Jr., Esq.
District Attorney, DeSoto Parish
42nd Judicial District, Louisiana

CONTENTS

FOREWORD
Robert Richardson, LRND Founder

Ever heard the saying, "Crazy like a Fox?" Well, maybe you've heard, "Don't let 'em outfox you." Both are age-old sayings that I can recall hearing most of my life.

My father once told me a story about a hunting expedition that he and a close friend went on. They packed food, camouflage clothing, dogs, weapons, and traps in hopes of catching the elusive red fox.

After two days of an exhausting game of hide-and-seek, my father and his friend had managed to catch not one, but three foxes, which was an above average performance for a couple of amateurs. However, his take on the story centered not around the three trappings but on the one that got away.

You see, following the first two catches, my dad and his buddy immediately bagged their bounty.

But when it came to the third, they left the fox unattended. One man went to get the camera from the truck and the other went to relieve himself.

When they returned to the site, all they found was a bloodstained number 2 victory trap and a fox's foot. The cunning creature has been known to gnaw his foot off to avoid capture, earning the title, "crazy like a fox."

Historically, the fox has been painted as a sly, skillful and amazingly intelligent animal. Folk tales about this mammal date as far back as the Middle Ages (about 500 AD to 1450 AD) with other tales like "Reynard the Fox," who used his charm and wit to avoid prosecution.

Thus, when Fox Rich mentioned her plans to write a "tell-all" and titling it, "The One that Got Away," I jumped at the opportunity to write the foreword.

Most of the stories and exploits found in books that grace our bookshelves today are borrowed, manufactured, or straight out fake. However, I know this story to be authentic and true of its author.

Fox Rich is certainly a very smart and crafty beautiful young vixen, much like the legends of old. As you read the pages of her story you will witness how she skillfully escaped the vicious clutches of "Dirty South" justice, permanently dismembered and scarred, but with her life in tow. You will glimpse how she is miraculously overcoming the odds of successfully rearing five boys single-handedly and how she's managing to come up in a downward economy.

When asked how she "done it," she candidly replies, "As for the charges I faced, I soon realized that the more we wiggle and fight, the webs we weave only become more entangled. So I assumed my share of the responsibility, accepted the charges, and took my lick."

Regarding the care for her young, she states boldly, "I don't sit around looking for pity or pats on the back from people, telling me how well I take care of my boys. Caring for my boys is not a contest I'm hoping to win. It's my duty…something I am supposed to do."

And as for her financial success, she exclaims, "When others played, I worked! When others slept, I worked. When others doubted, I worked. When others propositioned, I worked hard. And when others compromised, I worked even harder! Success is a lifetime pursuit, not a stopping point."

This body of work is a story written and shared in broad strokes about a tenacious young woman who, in the face of adversity and brutal opposition, refuses to let go of her goal to restore her family and realize her dreams.

"The One that Got Away" gives its readers the simple but hard truths about life. Today's youth need not learn life's most valuable lessons through trial and error when the universal principles to successful living are so evident and readily available from our adult population.

Thank God for Fox Rich.

LRND* proudly presents...Lessons LRND from "The One that Got Away."

Robert Richardson
LRND Founder
*Living Responsibly Never Deviating
Angola State Penitentiary

July 2009

MY CONTRITION

The early Christian Church practiced public confession and penance for sins as a part of the process of reconciliation. This show of contrition or sorrow for wrongs done was a critical part of the process of restoring one to the community.

After growing conscious of how everything we do affects everyone around us, I have longed to publicly apologize for the offense I committed over a decade ago. Before I go any further into sharing my life's experiences I feel I must start by apologizing to those I have offended.

To the victims of our offense and their families: We will never fully understand the level of trauma that our actions may have inflicted on you, but we pray that God has given you the peace and strength to overcome any harm we have caused. Our actions were foolish and self-centered. We focused only on our own plight, never once considering the other lives that would be so greatly impacted by our choices. Please forgive us.

To the citizens of Lincoln Parish, in particular the residents of Grambling, we offer our sincerest apologies for the damage that our actions may have wrought on your community. To the public officials responsible for carrying out justice in Lincoln Parish: we apologize for the utter disrespect and disregard that we displayed out of ignorance. We now understand how important it is that all our citizens feel some level of security and protection under the law, especially in the place they call home.

To my mother, family and friends: I know now that no man is an island and when someone you love hurts, it affects the whole. I am often still embarrassed by the shame and disgrace I brought upon those that love me. We are a strong family of great minds that identify with greater highs than the low I exposed us to. I thank God for your seeing the good in me even when I wasn't so good.

To my children: words are not enough to truly explain how deeply disappointed I am to know that by my very own actions I removed myself from caring for you. I can not change the past, but I work diligently everyday to be the best mother I can. Thank you for loving me inspite of my choices.

INTRODUCTION

Let me get it clear from the start:
I know I did not get away with anything--but my life.

It was the fall of 2007, and Tony Brown, the radio talk show host that broke the story of the Jena 6, had come up from Alexandria to Shreveport to meet with me. When he got here, he told me that they had re-arrested Michael Bell for parole violation, after the world had marched for his release. It immediately sent my mind racing, reflecting on my own brush with the law.

I thought about how my husband was still imprisoned on a 60-year sentence and his nephew on a 45-year sentence...both first time felony offenders, in a crime where no one was injured. Then I thought of myself, and how I had been home from prison for five years, and had been off parole for over a year. You see, initially, the prosecuting DA wanted to give me 40 years, then they offered my attorney 20; from there they went down to 12, and finally I took a plea bargain for two 7- year sentences and one 5-year sentence, to run concurrently.

With this in mind, I asked myself, "Why me? Why was I spared from the grueling clutches of our injustice system?" Then I heard my answer: "You were spared so that you could tell others." That is when I realized that I am to be a messenger for the people; to warn as many of my people as I can to stay clear of the system.

So I am writing these words in an effort to share my experiences with the masses, that the word may circulate throughout our community and we will be able to collectively: 1) decrease the number of our people who are entering the criminal justice system; 2) work to release those who have been unjustly imprisoned or excessively sentenced; and 3) break this vicious cycle of incarceration that is plaguing our community.

Before I found myself involved in the judicial system I thought that everyone in prison was totally guilty and that whatever time they received they deserved. As a college-educated woman who only had one relative on my mother's side that had ever been to jail, my exposure to the criminal justice system had been limited, to say the least.

I recall, very vividly, coming home from college to vote and voting in favor of two pieces of legislation that dealt with criminals. One was the habitual offender bill. The other required that violent offenders serve 85% of their time. It took me almost losing my life to realize the negative impact of what I had helped create.

Unfortunately, we can all think of a situation where we acted recklessly and placed ourselves in harm's way. It may have been changing lanes out of road rage, or driving after having too many drinks, having unprotected sex, avoiding the doctor when our bodies have given us warning signs, carrying too much weight on our frames, failing to exercise, excessively using over the counter drugs, the list goes on and on. Yet, the most valuable asset we have is our life. When we do not value it, we will more readily place ourselves in dangerous, unproductive situations that can leave us disfigured, distraught, and disdained.

My desire is to share my story with you in hopes that in some way, it will encourage you to not take for granted what has been given to us and to put our lives to the best possible use while we are here. Everyday with our actions, we are either choosing life or we are choosing death. Some choose a slow death and others move with haste and rush the possibilities of our demise.

At that point in my life, after having lost all that was dear and meaningful to me, and being left with only life itself, I made a decision to not only exist here with a beating heart, but to strive to live; to have life and have it more abundantly. I pray the same for you, the reader, that the words on these pages will connect with your inner being and you will reexamine your life and find its true value... priceless. May the universe move in your direction and love overflow and abound on your life's path.

Namaste.

Fox Rich

December 28, 2007

"Success is to be measured not so much by the
position that one has reached in life,
as by the obstacle which one has overcome while
trying to succeed."

Booker T. Washington

FROM THE BEGINNING
✤ Chapter One ✤

My beginnings may have been challenging, but they were never an excuse to fail. I was born Sibil Verdette Fox, on August 18, 1971. I came from people who had a strong desire to have something. I would like to welcome you to my story.

My mother's determination has been my greatest inspiration. She raised four children by herself on a public school teacher's salary: Sredni, Sharon, Sandra, and me, the youngest. While bearing this load, she also managed to finish college and went on to complete a master's degree and several hours toward a Doctorate. She worked diligently to provide for us. She seemed to always be working two jobs. I believe I get my tenacity from her.

From an early age she instilled in me a belief in the American Dream by telling me often, "Sibil, you can make it if you try." I believe it was her favorite mantra.

I don't know my biological father. The man I came to know as my father was a true hustler in every sense of the word. On one block, he owned a record store, a liquor store, a gas station and a pool hall. That might be where I get my entrepreneurial spirit from.

I grew up watching my daddy be the shot caller. At five years old, I was flying first class to see him in Texas. I had everything money could buy. I never knew he was not my real father until I made 18, and began asking questions.

We lived in Houston (where I was born) and Jasper, Texas. Then, while I was a toddler, my mother moved her children back to Shreveport. When I was three years old, she purchased our first home on Easy Street in the Stoner Hill section of the city.

My grandfather passed before I was born, but I knew my grandmother, Loy T. Autrey, who was a strong proponent of education. At a time when many blacks were taking advantage of factory jobs, she made sure all her children went to college. She also knew the importance of owning something. For years, until her death, she ran a neighborhood grocery store. That's where I would spend all of my days until heading off to Stoner Hill Elementary School.

I attended Broadmoor Middle School, and then went on to Caddo Magnet High, a performing arts school that brought out the best in me.

It was 1986, while in high school, that I met Robert Richardson, who said and did all the right things to win my attention and my heart. Our paths first crossed one day in November, after my girlfriend Wanda and I had cut morning classes at our home school. In desperate need of a ride to catch our last three classes, which were at Fair Park Medical Careers Magnet, she called Rob. He was one of her church members who was home on leave from the Navy. Upon her request he came through to help us out. Later that night he called me, and from there it was on. He was especially kind and caring and knew what he wanted out of life. I thought he was the kind of guy I wanted to spend the rest of my life with.

I graduated from high school prepared to enter college. In my family it was clearly understood that, just as there is high school after middle, there was college after high school. To help defray the cost of college, I joined the Navy Reserve. Upon completing basic training, I headed off to my mother's alma mater, Grambling State University, to pursue my degree in biology. At the urging of my mother, I went to college with the goal of becoming a doctor. She knew her child desired the finer things in life and at an early age recommended this field as one that would make it possible.

My college experience consisted of fun-filled days, in spite of being broke most of the time. I shared an apartment with my cousin Lil' Willie, who always had his partners over, drinking and 'cuing. In the last year of my undergraduate studies, after much persuasion from me, Robert joined me at Grambling. As a result, by the end of that school year, I was giving birth to our first son, Remington.

Unfortunately, by the time I completed my bachelor's degree, I realized that medical school was not something I wanted to pursue. Instead, I decided on a master's degree in Public Administration, with a concentration in Health Services.

Shortly before graduation, Robert and I had gone our separate ways...again. During this extended "off" period I entered into a relationship with the man who would become the father of my second child, Laurence. When disagreements turned physical, I left.

With my new credentials and my personal initiative, I set out to make my mark on the world. Even though I was not pleased with the idea of having two babies and two "baby daddies," having never been married, I was hopeful for a better tomorrow and the possibilities that still existed for building a family.

I was willing and ready to take on the world, with or without a man in my life.

Ready to take it to the next level.

And ohhhh what a level it was!

THE PURSUIT OF HAPPINESS
⚜ Chapter Two ⚜

May 26, 1999: I found myself facing up to 297 years in prison. I had reached the darkest day of my life, what some would call the point of no return. All because I had acted recklessly with the most valuable thing any human being could have while they walk on this planet, my gift of life.

Rewind: January 1997. I had graduated with my masters degree from Grambling State University and moved back home to Shreveport with my two sons, Remington, who was 3 ½ and Laurence who was almost one at the time, with one goal in mind...to build a better life for me and my boys.

That's when Robert, my high school sweetheart, on again off again boyfriend for ten years and father of my oldest son, re-enters my life and asks for my hand in marriage. Unlike many couples, we would have a "ready-made family." Robert had fathered a son, Mahlik, from a previous relationship, so together, we had three beautiful children. Therefore, we decided not to spend our money on a fancy wedding, trying to impress the public. Instead, we saved the wedding money for a down payment on our first home and eloped. Everything finally seemed to be coming together for me. I was the happiest I had ever been.

It was like a fairytale. The two of us headed off to Florida, and got married on April 24, 1997 at a small wedding chapel in Kissimmee. We spent the evening at Pleasure Island and then closed out the night by skydiving. We retuned home on April 30, and closed on our new house the same day. I felt a high like never before. In my opinion I had it all: a husband that loved me, a beautiful home, some adorable kids and big dreams for the future.

One of the greatest things I think Rob and I had in common, aside from our long history together, is that we both wanted to be entrepreneurs. We wanted our own business. While on the trip to Florida, we came up with a concept for what would be our first venture, a 'Hip-Hop' clothing store. Rob had spent a great deal of time on the East Coast and was introduced to small clothing stores that were carrying clothing lines by black designers referred to as Hip-Hop clothing shops. We thought it would be an ideal business because it would be a new concept in our market. The traditional business ventures that most folks we knew were starting consisted of car washes, beauty shops, and barber shops. We wanted to do something different, and this was it.

On May 24, 1997, we put a deposit on the location that was to become Culture…Shreveport's first Hip-Hop clothing store. Man, we stepped out! We were on a high to have a dream and watch it begin to unfold, and unfold so quickly. It was surreal, to say the least.

The next step was exposure. Since I had never experienced this concept, Rob wanted me to see what he was talking bout. We got a couple of magazines, the XXL and The Source, to find some locations closest to us that had what we were planning to implement. The closest shop, '4 da Soul N U', was in Houston. We called the store and made an appointment to meet with its owner, Lisa. Despite the negative stereotypes about black people being unwilling to support or assist each other, when we met, this sister poured information on us.

One of the most important pieces of intelligence we got was about the industry's main show. The Magic Show, the world's largest clothing show, is held twice a year in Las Vegas. The next one was a few months away, which gave us ample time to get there. Lisa insisted that you could not be in the clothing business and not attend The Magic, so Rob and I immediately took the info she gave, registered and made plans to attend the August 1997 Fall Magic Show.

In the meantime, Rob was determined for me to have a firsthand experience of his vision for our new venture, so off we went to the region of origin for Hip-Hop clothing, the East Coast. This was a new experience in itself. I had never been past the Mason-Dixon Line. To say I was excited is an understatement.

The first stop on this journey was Atlantic City and the historical Alexander's Hip-Hop Shop, where we were blessed on our path by a brother named Tito, the proprietor. He kicked us down with figures and sales expectations. But, by far, the most useful piece of advice that Tito passed on to a couple of overzealous entrepreneurs was "Just get open." Today, I still pass those words on to others that are engulfed in so many unimportant details that they lose sight of the main point. Just get open and you can grow from there.

Next, we hit a couple of spots in Philly that were nice. But the finale of the adventure was the Big Apple itself, with Dr. Jay's being one of the main attractions. We did not have a point of contact there, but we were able to get a feel for the layout and the possibilities of what was to come.

Now that I had a connection to our new project, the rest of the summer was spent actively marketing and promoting that we were gonna be the first to bring black designers and Hip-Hop clothing lines to Shreveport. We got T-shirts and fliers sporting our Culture logo and hit the ground running. We appeared on the front page of the business section of the Shreveport Times and made the cover of the Shreveport Sun, the local black newspaper. We commenced to hit every major event that came to town, from outdoor events to rap concerts. We even threw Patty Labelle one of our T-shirts during her concert here. If it was happening, we were there to let everyone know Shreveport was about to be on the map with the latest in Hip-Hop gear.

Before we knew it, it was Magic Show time.

With transportation supplied by my mother's Delta 88, housing accommodations provided by my sister Sharon, who lived in Vegas, and a few dollars in our pockets, we were off to the Magic fashion convention. I had visited Vegas before, but this trip was on a whole 'nother level. When we got there, we went to register and began making our way around, trying to connect with other people in the Hip-Hop clothing industry. We met the likes of Keith Perrin and Daymond John, the co-founders of FUBU, and Marc Buchanan, founder of Pelle Pelle. The group Naughty by Nature had launched a line as well, so they were there with a new group they were pushing. Even Shaquille O'Neal had a line called Twism.

We were about to be a part of a movement, getting in on a trend at the beginning stages. We spent the days at the convention networking and ordering gear and the nights at some of the fliest parties I've ever attended, with live performances by the likes of Fat Joe, Next, Naughty by Nature, and many more.

When we returned to Shreveport, we were on fire! We had a dream, and we were watching it unfold so beautifully. We set our minds on a goal and we went after it, believing that nothing was out of our reach.

And now we were down to the final stages, six weeks away from our scheduled opening date, and our plans were moving accordingly. Upon our return, we put the finishing touches on the store and set up a final meeting with our investor to receive our promised injection of working capital…and that's when things went wrong.

Real wrong.

His name was Travis and he was about to become one of my life's greatest teachers. He owned a truck refueling company that had many of the major contracts around town. I met him when I moved back to Shreveport after grad school. He was a prominent local businessman, and one of the few wealthy black men in town who would allow you to get close enough to have a conversation. After building a strong rapport with this brother and sharing my burning desire to own my own business one day, he told me that he would do what he could to help me. Once I worked out the details of a business venture, I was to let him know and he would invest.

As soon as the idea came forth, Rob and I presented a proposal to him. After months of working with his accountant, providing him with proof that this venture would be profitable, Travis gave us a verbal commitment to loan us $50,000.

Once we got back from the Magic Show, we met him at his office, as scheduled, to receive the promised funding. That is when Travis, in a very dismissive manner, informed us that he had changed his mind.

We were blown away, stunned and crushed. Damn! As Travis spoke those words to us, Rob and I looked at each other, devastated on the inside. Rob extended his hand to Travis and thanked him for making us stronger, because at that very moment, we both knew that we were about to sink or swim. I can't really put into words how we felt. We walked out of his office like zombies, with blank looks on our faces, in shock at what we had just experienced. In life, we cannot always control what others do to us, but we do have total control over how we respond. But I tell you I could have whipped his ass myself for playing with us like that.

Here we were, two inexperienced business people just getting our feet wet. We took the man at his word; after all, he had no reason to lie to us. So we never even thought to request that he put the commitment on paper. We had just planned to sign the contract for the terms of the investment and open our business. Now we know – if it didn't happen in writing, it didn't happen at all.

I can't say why Travis changed his mind. My only assumption is that when he made the offer to me, I was single and by the time I called in his favor I was married. I later met another woman he had mentioned helping. She, too, was in the clothing business. I stopped in her store by happenstance one day and after striking up casual conversation discovered we shared a mutual acquaintance, Travis. I asked her about her business venture with him and how it had gone. In so many words, she informed me that after he realized she was not going to be his "woman," he demanded his money back immediately and threatened to close her down. No booty, no bucks!

It was approximately four weeks before our scheduled opening date of October 1, 1997. How can one possibly describe the blow we had both just been dealt?

We had dreams as big as the Titanic, and just as it – we were going down fast.

THE FALL OF
SIBIL FOX RICHARDSON
⚜ Chapter Three ⚜

So now, here we were, in a space that neither of us had ever been in before; new couple, new house, new business. New dreams...totally crushed.

Robert came up with some suggestions on how we could get the help we needed. The first idea was a bank loan. Our credit was strong enough to buy a house, maybe some bank would find value in what we were trying to do and work with us on this project. After various attempts we discovered our credit was good enough to get a car loan or a home loan, but not a business loan. Every bank we went to turned us down.

Next, we thought, family. Surely without there being a business owner in the family since my grandmother, someone in our family would be willing to catch hold of this dream and help build it. Unfortunately, when you have a vision to accomplish something, it doesn't mean others are willing or even able to see it, because it is just that...your vision.

We were hurt. We knew that we were on to something big; a concept that could change the financial situation of our entire family, but we could not find anyone that would dream with us. All of the family members we asked said "No." Some even went as far as to say, "Hell, Nawh."

In the 90's in Shreveport, there were a few young men that we had gone to school with that had become successful entrepreneurs from street "pharmaceutical sales"…you feel me? So we presented them with the opportunity to transform their earnings and build new wealth. But with a concept as unique as ours, and much of their exposure being limited to Tommy Hilfiger and Polo, they could not see a business being profitable by selling clothing from black designers. After a few meetings with the company's "president", we realized we couldn't convince them to lend the necessary capital to make it happen.

As the days passed our anxiety grew. The deadline was upon us. October 1 was right around the corner. The clothing was on the way and we needed a way to pay for it.

After another unproductive meeting with another potential investor, Rob and I stopped at the park to breathe, smoke us one, and figure out what our next move would be. We rehashed all the previous options that we had pursued and tried to muster enough faith to create some new ones. But we were tapped, beginning to feel hopeless and destined for failure.

It was about this time, while we were trying to find the strength and courage to continue to pursue our dreams, that Rob jokingly reminded me of a conversation we had with a lifelong friend. We were discussing the movie, "Set It Off," when she declared, "Shit, I think I could do it." We both laughed at her because we didn't think she could get away with stealing candy from a baby. What we failed to realize is that with that thought, a seed had been planted. With that conversation, the course of our journey would change.

Like the Bible says, the power of life and death lies in our tongue. What we remembered as a joke that day began what we would come to accept as our only option to save our family…robbery.

I can't recall clearly what took place after that, but what I do know is that we thought we had come up with a solution to solve our existing problem. But with neither of us having participated in anything like this, we had to figure out how we would go about it. We spent the next couple of days driving around and scoping out a couple of possibilities.

Over the course of the next few days, we watched managers leave from businesses with money bags. We looked at a couple of convenience stores and that is when it hit us: we needed $50,000, and none of the potential prospects we had been looking at would have that kind of money on site. The only place that would have that kind of loot on hand would be...a bank. In addition to that, we realized that *if* we were caught, (which we really had not given any thought to), the charge and jail time would be the same. So if we were gonna do it, we might as well *"go for the gusto."* That's when we decided we would rob a bank.

The next issue was what bank and the method. We looked at a couple of banks around Shreveport, and then I recalled hearing about a bank robbery that occurred while I was at Grambling State. When I was in grad school someone had hit the Grambling Federal Credit Union, which was located next door to the police station. I told Robert that if they got robbed while the bank was next door to the police and they never caught the perpetrators, then that would be an easy lick.

A few days later, we got up and drove down to Grambling, Louisiana to scope out the credit union. When we got there, we discovered that the bank was no longer next door to the station, but around the corner now, which in our minds would make it an even easier target. If somebody, we thought, could rob the bank while it was right next door to the police station and get away, certainly we could pull off a heist around the corner.

We went down a few more times; I guess just trying to build up the nerve to pull it off. After checking out the scene, Rob decided that instead of going in by himself he needed someone to go in with him. But who? With all of the adrenaline following in me, I asked Rob if he wanted me to go in with him. He quickly, in a sharp, decisive tone, said, "No!"

Who did we know that would be willing to take this type of risk? He tossed some names around of people he knew, that if given the right scenario, just might consider it. Then he thought of his nephew who had just moved down from Kansas, trying to escape some trouble he had gotten into, and decided to pitch the hustle to him.

Ontario had just made his 21st birthday and had no real plans for life. He was a young man, busy trying to find himself and his place in this big world. And with two small kids, and no viable skills or trade, he was in as desperate a state of mind as we were. After hearing from his uncle what would be our "come up"...Ontario was in.

The plan was coming together, so we thought. We knew what we would do, who would be involved, and what our target would be. Now, it was just a matter of how and when.

If I had to guess, I would say our knowledge of the best way to rob a bank probably came from television. We had not done any detailed research on our own. And with our opening deadline fast approaching, we felt that we were pushed for time. With Ontario now on board, we decided to take another trip to Grambling, so he could see what we saw.

From there, it was on.

SET IT OFF: THE HEIST
❦ Chapter Four ❦

On Monday, September 15th, we took a test run to Grambling. We knew we would be leaving early the next morning, so we let the boys spend the night at Robert's sister's house. We also asked her to trade cars with us, secretly trying to make sure we disguised ourselves. Now, how the hell we expected to use a three-cylinder Hyundai as a getaway ride, I will never know. But what I do know is if Rob's poor sister only had a clue of what we were trying to use her car for...to this day, I bet she still would like to give me and her brother a swift kick in the ass for pulling that shit.

The big day came, Tuesday, September 16, 1997—the day we carried out our "Operation Desperation." We woke up at 5:00 am, and began to put in motion our plan to "get money," something that is driving so many urban youth today. I cannot even begin to describe the thoughts that were running through my mind, knowing what we set out to do on that morning.

We arrived in Grambling at about seven o'clock that morning. We wanted to catch the bank as soon as it opened. When we got in town, headed toward the bank, we were behind a school bus that had failed to stop before it crossed the railroad tracks. That's when the driver began to back up to correct her error and smashed into the front of our car. Bammmm! We got out of the car, nervous as shit and saw that the whole front end of the car had been damaged. We called the police so that we could get a report. I was shaking in my boots. Here we are, planning a heist and having to call the police to the scene of an accident that we were involved in. I was paranoid when the cop arrived and began to move around the vehicle, inspecting it. My mind was focused on the possibility of him finding the firearm that was in our possession.

The whole process took about forty-five minutes. He took my license and said I could come by the police station to pick it up and get my copy of the police report.

We drove off, and as I looked at Robert, I was thinking, "Now what?" At that point, Robert felt like we had an even greater reason to proceed. "The car is wrecked. How will you get away?" I asked. He said, "Don't worry about that. I will get a teller's car."

"So you really want to go ahead and do this?" I asked.

"We don't have a choice," he replied.

That's where we were wrong. No matter what situation you may find yourself in, you must know that you *always* have a choice. None of us really wanted to do it. This type of behavior was beneath us, yet none of us could muster up the courage to back away. We all felt we were in too deep to turn around.

I dropped Rob and Ontario off in the woods next to the bank. Then I headed to higher ground and posted up to lookout, or "watch the bus," as they say in the streets. After I watched them enter the bank, I made my way to the police station to get my driver's license. Certainly with us being in town pulling this caper, I did not want my identification hanging out at the police headquarters. I got one block from the station when I saw two police cars flying past me, lights flashing. Oh my God! I called Rob, screaming, "Get out! Get out!" I proceeded to the station, went to the window, got my license, shaking like a leaf on the inside, and then drove to the nearby town of Ruston to wait for word…

Some time had passed and I figured I would try to slide back in the vicinity to see if I could find out what had happened. Did they get out in time? Did they get caught? Were they okay? As I was coming around a curve, headed back into Grambling on the old highway, an ambulance passed me. My heart dropped. I burst into tears. Did they get shot? What have we done? Then I thought, "Oh my God, what if they shot someone?" We had not given any consideration to these possibilities. I began to shake, crying uncontrollably. How ugly was this really about to turn out to be? Has someone been hurt? I never contemplated violence…but then how can you expect to take something from someone and not use force? My God, what have we gotten ourselves into?

In a state of panic, I contacted a good friend who worked at Grambling, and asked her to come and get me. I was in uncharted territory. I had never been on the run before, but my senses told me they would probably be looking for me and I needed to park my sister-in-law's car.

My friend came to Ruston and picked me up. After seeing the ambulance, I needed to get back to Grambling and try to find out what happened. I hid down in her car as she drove back by the bank. I needed to know if anybody had been hurt. Had they been caught or did they get away? As we passed the crowd and confusion, she said she saw one of them in the police car. Could one of them have been in the ambulance, I wondered? I was breathless.

I rode with her back to Ruston, so I could figure out what my next move would be. One thing I knew for sure was that I needed to get my ass out of town as fast as I could. So I did just that. Wrecked car and all, I got on the road and headed for Shreveport.

Filled with fear, I was hoping to make it home on what seemed like the longest trip of my life. I left home with my husband and his nephew, and now I would return alone…if I was lucky. The chances of encountering a roadblock on the 70-mile stretch home were too real to be ignored. With every exit I passed, I thought they would be there waiting on me. I was frozen thinking every car in my mirror might be a pursuing cop.

After a daunting journey, I made it, thank God! It was late in the evening of one of the worst days of my life when I arrived at Robert's sister's house, Rose. I knew I would have a lot of explaining to do. For one, her car was 'tore up'; and two, I left with her brother and her nephew, yet I was retuning alone and late for picking up Laurence.

For the life of me I cannot recall what lie I had prepared to tell Rose when I got there, but by the time I got out of the car I discovered things had already broken loose. She greeted me with, "The man from the FBI just called here looking for you. They say they have a warrant out for your arrest and you need to come back to Ruston and turn yourself in."

My mind wondered, "How did they get Rose's number and how did they know I would be there?" "Shit," I thought, "If they want me, they better come get me." I gathered up the baby and tried to tune out Rose as she continued to seek answers. Then the phone rang. Rose answered it, and then handed to me. Did my ass say I was scared? I was shitting bricks.

I got on the phone, "Hello," I said. Then the voice on the other end introduced himself as FBI Agent Harry Deal, who was handling the investigation of the robbery of the Grambling Credit Union. He informed me that he had both Robert and Ontario there with him. He went on to say, "I need you to get back down here and turn yourself in." I said, "What do you mean? I don't know what you are talking about." He responded, "You can stop lying. Rob has told us everything." Then he put Rob on the phone.

Initially I was delighted to hear his voice. I had been worried that something had happened to him. On the other hand, I was disappointed because every hope that he had gotten away was now thrown out the window. Not only had he been caught, the FBI claimed to know everything.

The agent again instructed me to head back down to Ruston for questioning. With little or no knowledge of the law, I told him, "I don't know what you are talking about, but I don't have a problem coming down with my attorney." I later learned that the FBI agents had told Robert that if he told what they needed to know, they would not pursue me and they would work to make sure they got him a good deal.

Some police officers use lines like these to get suspects to cooperate, knowing that they have no intention of honoring their word.

I traded cars with Rose, and then headed to the school to pick up Remington. At a ripe four years old, he was wise beyond his years. When he got in the car, the first words out of his mouth were, "Where is my daddy?" Robert usually picked him up everyday. So for me to show up, he knew something was not right.

I was raised by a very matter-of-fact type of woman. My mother was straightforward with us, and I tried to raise my boys the same way. So I gave him the truth: "Your daddy is in jail," I said. Instantly, he broke into a loud yell and cried, "Noooo." I boohooed. Here he was, just getting accustomed to having his father in the home with him again, no sooner than that, he was gone.

I could see the initial stages of all the pain yet to come from this horrible set of decisions. I thought once more, "Oh my God, *what have we done?*"

I dashed by our house to pick up a few things, because I knew that until I could find a lawyer, I would be hiding out. I thought of all the different people they could send after me: Shreveport Police, the marshals, the Sheriffs, the FBI. My mind raced. I felt like it was hunting season and I was the only game in town. I decided that I would spend the night at my mother's house; hopefully they would not look for me there. It was not the best hide out, but the only one I could get without any money. However, the next problem was the person who would be at my mother's house…you guessed it, my mother…who doesn't miss a thing.

Now, how do you begin to explain to your mother that you and your husband just robbed a bank, and you are on the run? I believe I told her that Robert was in jail for robbery. The rest is foggy, probably because I want to forget. The only part of her response I remember is something like, "That is some bullshit. You all did not have that shit to do." It was one day that I could not wait to see come to an end.

I slept that night with anticipation that, at any moment, someone would bust through the door, coming to pick me up. Needless to say, that doesn't make for a good night's sleep.

THE MORNING AFTER
✠ Chapter Five ✠

Some situations can be fixed with a "morning after" pill. However, this was not one of them. We had started something we couldn't stop. My mama says, "Shit is easy to get into, but hard to get out of."

The games had begun. The chase was on, and I was running for my life. I rose early that morning. Actually, the only sleep I got felt like a drunken stupor. I knew a few things I needed to do: the first was to get the kids off to school; the second was to find me a lawyer.

As soon as I got the boys off, I thought about the ex-husband of one of my girlfriends, who was an attorney in Lincoln Parish. Rick Gallot was his name. I called information, got his number, and put in a call to his office to see if he could help me. He set up an appointment for me, and said in the meantime he would make some phone calls to get more information. He called me back later that day and confirmed that a warrant had indeed been issued for my arrest on the charges of armed robbery (see affidavit for arrest warrant).

On that Friday, September 18, I went down to meet Rick at his office and gave him the gory details of what we had done. He told me to see what I could do to get some bond money together, because from what he had gathered the judge would was looking to set my bond at $50,000, ironically, the same amount we were trying to get. I would need about $1,200 to post my bond when we went to the detention center to turn myself in. The magical date for my arrest was set for September 26th.

I got back to Shreveport and shared what I had learned with my mother. (One beautiful thing about a real mother is that no matter had badly you may mess up, they will stand by your side, and I thank God I have a real mother). She, in turn, called the "head" of our family. I believe there is that one person in each family that everyone can, and does, turn to in their time of need. That person in my family is my Aunt Coral Jean. Based on my mother's commitment to pay her back, Aunt Coral Jean loaned me $1,200 for my bond.

The morning of September 26th, my mother took off work and went down to Ruston with me. I reported to Rick's office. He informed me that he had spoken to the DA's office and the judge had agreed to release me on a signature bond, meaning I would not have to secure my bond with cash. It would be after lunch when I would report to the detention center in Lincoln Parish to get arrested. The fingerprinting…the mug shots…Man! This was a whole new state of affairs for me. As I stated before, my interaction with the judicial system had been so limited up to this point that I knew nothing.

With two college degrees, I still felt like an illiterate as I listened to the legal jargon that was being tossed around. To me, it was like they were speaking a foreign language. I consider myself to be a well-rounded person. There are not many situations that I can't at least feel my way through. But in this system, I was lost. About the only thing I had done right was to shut my mouth until I had legal representation. Unfortunately, that is not something many people under duress remember…You do have the right to remain silent.

Once I got somewhat of a handle on the situation, the next thing I needed to get clear on was how, after all of this, would I be able to save our dream? With the tremendous fall we just took…now, more than ever, I had to find away to make it happen. Not having to post a bond, I asked my mother's permission to use the money from Aunt Coral Jean to pay the lease on the building. Continuing to believe in me, even after I had just messed-up majorly, she agreed. With that money, I could pay the rent and buy myself some time to figure out what would be next. But the one thing I knew for sure, if I didn't know anything else, was "we couldn't quit now!"

From here, legal matters began to move quickly. With Rick also representing Robert and Ontario, a court date was set for all three of us. In the meantime, I worked on a way to get Culture up and running.

To me and Rob, Culture would not just be the first store to sell black designers in the South; it would be a movement, a place where people could come and vibe with each other on elevating our community. In addition to the clothing, we where going to have books and art and dancers to bring the clothing to life.

That is how I met Aiesha. While marketing and promoting the store, Rob and I connected with Aiesha and her husband at one of our events. They were interested in our project and Aiesha, who had recently lost her job, put her name in the hat for some employment. Knowing I needed some help now, for real, I gave her a call. When I contacted her, I told her what I was up against and she, in turn, told me the issues she was dealing with. She and her man were on the rocks, and she was trying to move out.

In my efforts to save the store, I had moved all my belongings out of our new home and into the warehouse behind the store. I rented the house out and cut my overhead. I extended an invitation to Aiesha to join me. My offer was that we all could live in the store. In exchange for her help in running the store, she could have a free place to lay her head, until she got on her feet and figured out her next move. It was a plan that would move us closer to getting the capital needed to open.

With Robert's guidance from the jail cell via collect calls, we devised a plan to rise from the ashes. The vehicle we created would be hosting parties. It was something Rob did while living on the East Coast. I had thrown a few college parties and with the space of the warehouse, we would have the needed venue. I also worked on getting lines of credit from clothing companies that needed their inventory in our region.

Meanwhile, I had a pre-sentencing investigation and preparation for a court date. We were scheduled for arraignment in mid October.

In most court cases, upon first appearing, the traditional "not guilty" plea is entered; but based on the recommendation from our attorney, we all entered guilty pleas. Within a matter of days we were before the judge, preparing to receive our sentences. Robert had been calling me, sharing different insights he had been receiving in jail that made him feel Rick did not have our best interests at heart. He cited the fact that Rick was the alderman for the town of Grambling. This, he thought might be a conflict of interest, with him representing both us and the city we committed the offense in.

Second, he was concerned about how quickly we were being rushed through the system. For others locked up with him, the state was electing to repeatedly continue their matters for months at a time. Most attorneys, as I understand it, consider it a strategy to put some time between the incident and all parties involved before moving to resolve the matter. As the old saying goes, time heals all wounds. Enough time would serve to cool the tempers of all those involved. So he decided, and I agreed, that we needed to withdraw our guilty pleas and opt for another lawyer.

The judge agreed to this withdrawal based on his own observation. And with this, we fell deeper into the system. Certainly with the DA's office thinking this was one more case they had laid to rest, and now here it was, back on their plates...needless to say, they weren't too pleased. I believe this is the point we began to piss them off.

Culture's initial opening date was supposed to be October 1, 1997. However, using what we had, we were able to get the store opened for business on November 1st. We followed what I learned from Tito at Alexander's Hip-Hop Shop, who said it best: "Don't worry 'bout all that stuff, just get open."

I have found that, many times, it is not that we lack everything we need to have in order to realize our dreams. What I think happens is that we end up focusing all of our energies on what we don't have, and therefore are not able to put to use the resources that are readily available to us. This causes us to operate from a spirit of "lack" instead of what each of us truly are...abundant beyond measure. When you've got life, your health, and your strength, you've got it all.

On opening day, my mother's words rang through my head, "Y'all did not have that to do."

Robert could have been there with me to celebrate what we had achieved, if only we could have seen past the brief storm that we were going through; if we had trusted that the same God that gave us the vision for this business would be the same God to assist us in manifesting it. "It" was the grand opening of Culture clothing store, Shreveport's original Hip-Hop clothing shop. Even though the store was not loaded down with inventory, we were open and made $267.00 on opening day.

Now, with one great feat under my belt, I still had a life-threatening challenge ahead of me. I was hanging on an armed robbery charge, while my new husband and his nephew where sitting in the parish jail for the same thing.

We went through several thousands of dollars on attorneys and phone bills, trying to find some help from within the system to find our way out the system. By February of 1998 I was barred from visiting Robert at the parish jail.

I re-enrolled in grad school at Grambling, so I could continue to get my loan check, you know how it is! One night, when I got out of class, I was pulled over and arrested. Without even running my driver's license, the officer said there was a warrant out for my arrest for issuing worthless checks. I had not gotten in the car good before I was stopped, so he had to have been waiting for me. I had no clue of what they were talking about. When we got to the police station he pulled out some paperwork that showed I had a bounced check for maybe $25. It was from a grocery store from years earlier that I was totally unaware of.

Boy, they had gone and done some digging on me! Before this situation, I had been arrested once, but Lord, now it seemed like every time I turned around they were there! At this point , the only ways Robert and I could communicate were by mail and by phone. With trying to keep the business open, in one month we had a $3,000 phone bill.

The store was doing well and we began to look for other ways to generate revenue. Having this big warehouse in the back, we came up with the idea of Culture's Underground Comedy Club and put on our first show. I guess I had an eye for talent, because in my pursuit of comedians, I went down to Houston's Jus' Joking comedy club. That is where I met the very funny Thomas Myles, who is now known, on the nationally syndicated Steve Harvey morning radio show, as co-host, Nephew Tommy. That ended quickly, however, after someone called the fire department and told them we were not in code compliance. On to the next plan.

Before I knew it, summer was over and Remington was off to kindergarten. Such a beautiful understanding spirit he was. An old soul locked in a young boy's body.

We got our fall lines in and began preparing for the Christmas shopping season. Nothing was going on with our case, except the monthly court appearances that they make you do. They drag you back and forth every month, like they just want to remind you that they are about to get you and you are on a short leash. When we would go, boy I tell you, it would break my heart to see Ontario and Robert just chained up like mad dogs, and to know, in the depths of my mind, that if we didn't get some resolve, my ass was next.

In October I got a phone call that really touched my heart. The president of the Shreveport Chamber of Commerce called me to tell me that I had been selected to receive the "Rising Young Entrepreneur Leader of the Year Award." Wow! What a compliment! Me, receiving an award from business leaders in my city…what an honor!

Almost a year had passed since we had caught our charge. Aiesha met a dude, fell in love and moved out of the store to be with him. The boys and I continued to rent out our home and live in the back of the store. We had mastered operating without a shower or hot water. The building had all-electric appliances except for the hot water heater. I never could put aside the money to pay the commercial fee for the gas deposit. So, for hot water, we had to boil. I took wash-offs and put the boys in a bucket in the sink. The building had a small kitchenette and a few rooms, one of which we used as our bedroom. We used the bunk beds the boys had, and our sleeper sofa, and made it work. Like my mama said, "You can make it if you try."

The building itself was huge. It was so big that I would get scared sometimes there alone. One night, the boys and I were sleeping, at about 3:00 in the morning, when I heard glass crash. I jumped up and ran into the storefront. Someone was breaking in the store! I was scared as shit and mad at the same time, because my ass did not have any insurance. The next day I got the window fixed and replaced the stolen merchandise, only to turn around and get hit again two days later, then again the next night. I was traumatized and defeated. I am bringing business to the inner city, and yet someone wants to take from me. I don't have much. Why did they not choose one of the big department stores? Within five days, I was robbed three times.

Then I thought about the laws of the universe. You reap what you sow. Not only did we decide to rob a bank, but the only black bank in North Louisiana. Like our burglar, we, too, had preyed on our own kind. I couldn't be as mad at my robber because I had fallen to the same low way of thinking.

Robert had been trying for awhile to get me to move into the mall. At this point I think I was ready to try something new. And we did. On November 1, 1998, Culture Urban Outfitters opened in South Park Mall. Business was good. The market had finally become hip to urban gear. Now, it was in demand and we had the supply.

After making it through the holiday season, Rob and I started working toward bonding him out. He thought that with his feet on the ground he could help work our cases and assist me in running the store. He put a plan together that reduced his bond from $300,000 to $150,000 and with $9,000 cash, we could get him out.

He talked to a lot of different bondsmen in that parish, but none of them would touch him. One day while at court, a bondsman I knew from Grambling gave me the card of someone who he thought would help. And like magic, with money from my spring student loan and monies from Culture, I had what I needed to move him. I met with them on Friday and on Tuesday, February 2, 1999 we were picking Rob up from the detention center. It was surreal. Rob was coming home. You know where the first stop was once we got into town don't you? You guessed it…the bedroom.

I had made some great strides for us while Rob had been gone. Aside from the opening and relocation of the business, I also secured a spot as the host of one of the local television programs, and had a taping on the day of his return. Additionally, I was writing a weekly column for The Times, and had made my way on to the public speaking circuit. People wanted to hear what I had to say, and I wanted to tell them. My first engagement was at the Jackson Heights projects for their Black History program. It was a glorious first day home.

At the end of February I got a late-night call from my attorney's office. They told me I had a court appearance the following morning. I thought something was suspicious about this. From the last time I had gone to court I wasn't scheduled to return until sometime in March. We could smell a rat.

I was pissed off at my attorney for pulling what I felt was a last-minute shenanigan on me, plus our business had paid to take

Remington's class on a field trip to Sci-Port, a local science center, and I was to chaperone. After the monkey wrench had been thrown in our plans, we decided that I would go to my court date and Robert would do the field trip. That settled, I began to figure maybe this attorney was not working on my behalf either.

When I got there, everything was already in play. As soon as they called me up, they increased my bond to 100,000 dollars and locked me up. Now, I was the one making collect calls from the parish jail. I called the store and sent the word out to Rob..."They got me." Determined to come to my rescue, by 10:00 that night, Rob had put together my release with the help of my mother, Aunt Coral Jean, and Aunt Pinkie. He later told me that he was motivated by the fact that he did not want to have to explain to our boys why I was not coming home. Man, this chase was getting mad!

As you can imagine, with Rob having been gone for a year-and-a-half, we missed a lot of grown folk's time, which led to the next set of events. It was the end of March when I realized that I had not had a visit from my monthly friend. We got a pregnancy test, and as you can imagine, Fertile Myrtle was knocked-up. Excited, because we wanted another child, but depressed because we did not want one under these conditions...we were still mentally on the run for our lives. It wasn't long before a bad case of morning sickness set in and left me unable to even get out the bed. At this time, Rob was basically running everything.

I tried desperately to pull myself together because Rob needed my help. We had put together a big comedy show for Good Friday weekend, in April that Adele Givens would headline and Nephew Tommy would host. Brotha Man, from the Martin Lawrence television series, would also be making an appearance. It was to be our legal fundraiser.

Show night came. The house was packed from the front to the back. I stood on the sideline, talking to Adele about her career and my desire to speak, when she gave me some words of advice that I've held on to. She said, when she decided she wanted to do comedy, she took every opportunity that came along to take the stage and make people laugh. "With a crowd like the one you have here tonight," she said, "you should be speaking. Don't wait on an invitation; take the 'mic' as often as you can." This was wisdom that I would definitely use later on.

With the party over and a new baby on the way, we turned our attention back to the store. We headed out to the East Coast to cop some more inventory. When we got back to Shreveport, we were in for a rude awaking. The trial that had been put off for almost two years was now set for May 20th...and we were no more prepared for it than a sixth grader is for medical school. We were in trouble.

THE WEB OF JUSTICE
✠ Chapter Six ✠

Right here is where things really turned ugly. This part is by far the hardest to revisit and summarize.

After he sat in jail for nearly a year and a half, now that Robert had bonded out, the DA's office was ready to proceed. During this entire experience, my mother kept saying, "Sibil, keep your ass from down there. Stay out of those folks' faces," but I couldn't hear her. Robert and I had gotten into this mess together and my conscience did not want him to feel abandoned. Robert's mother passed when he was five, his father was way up in age, and his sisters and brothers were spread across the nation. I felt I was all he had at the bleakest point in his life.

On Wednesday, May 20th, they started the jury selection. The attorney we had hired on a temporary basis to handle Robert's bond reduction was a college boyfriend of mine who had just passed his bar exam. He had never had a trial before, so it goes without saying, he was totally inexperienced. Now don't get me wrong; he was a smart brother, one whose intelligence I've always admired, but he lacked the experience and connections needed to help see us through this storm. Our plans were to use him until we had made some more money and could hire effective counsel.

Hiring a lawyer, we learned, was more than just giving someone a retainer. When looking for counsel, you must choose someone who has a working relationship with those that are prosecuting you.

Murphy was an outsider; a young, black, male attorney from Baton Rouge. He had no established relationship with these people, so aside from professional courtesy, they had nothing for him. When hiring a lawyer, you are not just buying representation, you are paying for relationships.

With this in mind, Robert attempted to have Murphy removed from our case, but after numerous delays and attorney changes, the judge was not hearing it. We would be Murphy Bell's first trial case, and if we thought we were in trouble before, now we knew we were buried for real.

After sitting through two days of pretrial stuff, I was in awe at how the judge ruled everything in the prosecutor's favor. Don't ask me why I was surprised. Remember, I am the same person who thought justice was blind, before I became entangled in her web. One evening, after we had finished the day's proceedings, the district attorney walks in, and with my mom's hot headedness, I said to him, "When I grow up to be a big girl, I'm going to have me a judge in my hip pocket." Did I say I had just put the last nail in our coffin? They were already sick of us. Now how, in my ignorance, could I be stupid enough and disrespectful enough to address, in a haughty manner, the very person pushing my prosecution? My grandmother would say, "Damn fool!"

By Friday, the jurors had been selected. We met with Murphy and went over who they were and what their various attitudes may be about this case. Our lives were passing before us fast, and we needed some more time...Robert had an idea that maybe some ailment could give us a couple of more days and then we could implement the second phase of his plan...talking to a juror.

While living in New Jersey, Robert had served on a criminal case as a juror. One day, after court had adjourned, the defendant pulled him and another juror to the side and shared with them his side of what happened in his case. With the DA trying to make us look like professional career criminals, he thought that if we could talk to one of the jurors, they would see us for who we really were: a young couple who had fallen prey to desperation.

On the day the trial was set to start, Robert and I reported to the hospital, instead of the courthouse. When we first arrived, they took our information and told us to have a seat. The night before, we had asked my sister, who was a nurse, for advice on what medical complaints are hardest to detect. She said that chest pains were one of the top ones. While Robert was reporting this ailment to the nurse, a big, burly black sister started hollering out for help. All of the attention Robert was about to get shifted to the woman. I hunched Robert and said, "You better do something, the judge is not going to understand us 'sitting' in the emergency room." With that suggestion, Rob let out a loud yell, grabbed his chest, and began a descent to the floor. The male nurse came and caught him. Out of the corner of my eye, I got a glimpse of the older woman. She was frowned up and rolling her eyes at him, as if to say, "Gott damn it! Don't be taking my spotlight." If I weren't in so much trouble I would have cracked my side. Boy, we still get a laugh about that one to this day.

We had the doctor call and tell the judge where we were. The day was spent in the emergency room with threatening phone calls coming in to the doctor from the judge. After a day full of testing we were released late that evening and were off to the next mission. With the names of two prospective jurors, we went home, picked up the boys and headed to Ruston to try and save our necks.

The first juror we went to see was a man who was courteous and curious. He listened to what we had to say for a brief moment, and then we departed. The next juror we wanted to talk to lived way up in the woods, in a small town we had never heard of, called Hico. It was further than we had expected.

By the time we made it to her house, it was about 9:00 pm and pitch black dark. I told Robert to stay in the car with the boys and I would knock on the door. Seeing a man this late at night could scare her, and we did not want that. When she opened the door, she had a small child in her arms. As I introduced myself, she began to say, "No. They told us not to talk to you all." I responded, "Yes ma'am," still asking for a minute of her time, but she refused. Before we left, I respectfully asked her to not tell anyone that we had been there and then we left. By the time we made it back to Shreveport, it was about eleven o'clock, and we were whipped in more ways than one. As we laid down to bed Robert's last words were, "Lord, please hold that lady's tongue," and with that, we fell asleep.

The next morning, Tuesday, May 26, 1999, we made it to Ruston for court. When we arrived — you guessed it — we were immediately separated and rushed into the courtroom. After some questioning, I was taken to a holding area and placed under arrest. It did not take a rocket scientist to figure out that the female juror had called the Sheriff. Speaking of which, the Sheriff himself read me my rights. As he was doing so, I recall thinking, "Hurry up, so that I can post my bond and figure my way out of this mess." At about that point, he got to the part that said, "Your bond is set at half a million dollars." It was then that I knew I would be spending my first of many nights in jail.

The court-appointed attorney came in and spoke with me. Then the Sheriff and the Warden personally drove me to the detention center to book me...again. Once there, I heard the Warden tell the jailor to place me on suicide watch in isolation. "She's in so much trouble," he said, "I believe she may try and kill herself."

In the isolation room I had nothing. No window to the outside. No clock, no TV, no book, no nothing. I believe it was the first time in my life I had ever been in solitude. Let me tell you, with no access to the outside world, being alone with nothing but yourself will either make you go crazy or go within. I knew that things were very bleak for me. I worried about Robert and Ontario. What did they do? Did they continue with the trial?

As I lay there, pregnant, in a suicide holding cell, I had to ask myself, what were my options? I could face the music and suffer the consequences of my poor decision making, or I could check out. That is when I heard something that I had never heard before. It was the pounding of my heart, pumping the blood through my veins. And it was at this moment I chose to live. Life is indeed a choice, and we choose on a daily basis whether we want to live or die.

I was not sure how this was going to pan out. I was in so much trouble, I could not even see straight. I couldn't even breathe. But what I did know is that I was gonna stick it out. I had a brief taste of what making good choices felt like. Now I was suffering the initial consequences of what I had created, but I was willing to pay the piper. I knew, in my heart, I had a reason for living. When I thought about the fact that some divine intelligence had my heart beating without any direction from me, and my lungs inflating and deflating without my instruction, it made me know that my life and my purpose for being here was so much bigger than me.

The next morning a guard came by and told me what had transpired with Rob. He said that they had kept them in court until 3:00 am, when the jurors came back with a guilty verdict. I was also informed that some time that morning I would have a chance to meet with my attorney.

The first words out of Murphy's mouth at that meeting with Rob and I were, "Do you all know how much trouble you are in?" I looked at Rob, he looked at me, and we looked at Murphy. Lo and behold, the jury tampering charge was the same amount of time as the time for the crime the jury was convened for.

There are only two jury tampering cases on record in Louisiana's history, one in 1938, and ours. In this case armed robbery was 5 to 99. With the jury tampering charges added, we were looking at a total of 297 possible years behind bars.

I looked at Rob and said, "What have we done?" (In my mind we had destroyed our lives; with our bare hands, we had just ripped them up.) Rob looked at me, and said, in the same strength I've always found comfort in, "We're gonna be alright." I did not know how in the hell we would be alright, or even what alright was, but when he spoke those words, they were just what I needed to carry on. Still, I knew "alright" would not be coming any time soon.

Since I had not talked about cutting my throat, the Warden eventually moved me in to population. Boy, it was like everybody at the jail had heard and was waiting for me to arrive on the cell block.

As soon as I got in the door, I reached out to the world; I could finally make a phone call. Like most folks in trouble, you know who I called first…Mama. My mama's biggest concern was what to do about the store. As soon as she returned home from court, the day we were arrested, she began to move everything out of the store. She was ahead of the game. When we spoke, she even lamented not having $56,000 to bond me out. I was touched that she had even given it some thought. Talk about a mother's love.

We had sunk to an all new low in the system. What we believed was an attempt to save our lives, others viewed as us trying to beat the charge. How do we make it back from here?

CONCEPTION OF A MIRACLE
⚜ Chapter Seven ⚜

I was three months pregnant and big as a house. I was trying to get acclimated to my new status in life as a prisoner and all that goes along with it: the poor tasting food, that I could not seem to get enough of (I had never been so hungry in my life); the fire retardant mattress and pillows that forbid a good night's sleep; the isolation from the outside world, and my plethora of new roommates that on the outside would not have been my preference. At some point I realized that, in the midst of fighting for my life, I had not yet received the medical care I needed for the new life inside of me.

I think I had been in the parish jail for about two weeks when they finally got me to the hospital for a prenatal appointment. I can't recall many details from certain parts of that jail stint, but one day that is etched in my psyche is my trip to E. A. Conway hospital, in Monroe, to see the obstetrician.

Before we left the parish jail, they handcuffed and shackled me, and assigned two armed guards to serve as my escort. I don't know what they thought this big, pregnant woman was capable of. I guess they did not want to find out either. When we arrived at the hospital and got out of the car, I could see the faces of all the people waiting outside the building, staring at me, while at the same time trying not to look. If I had said "boo," I probably would have scared them.

It was one of the most humiliating events of my life. I felt like I was being paraded around like a captured slave. In my mind, I imagined what my ancestors must have felt like, being poked and prodded, and placed on exhibition in the nude on slave auction blocks. And that is what gave me strength: I figured if they were able to maintain their dignity, in spite of the inhumane treatment they endured through no fault of their own, then certainly I could continue to hold my head up, knowing I had put myself in this trick bag.

We made our way to the prison ward. I did not even know these existed. That is where I waited until the doctors were ready for me. Trip part about it, is that the prison ward area was also the labor ward for prisoners. It was cold and uninviting. I had to have delivered one of the hardest prayers I ever prayed, "Lord please help me, thank you for granting me a bond reduction. Thank you for not letting me bring my baby into the world under these conditions," I said this prayer over and over again with tears flowing from my eyes.

One of the cruelest things I have found in this system is its treatment of pregnant women. When an incarcerated woman delivers a baby, they actually handcuff her to the bed. Then, after delivery, her time with the child is limited.

Lord, I knew I had done wrong, but all I could do was begin thanking God for the miracle in all of this that He would grant me. Soon the guards came and escorted me to see the doctor, there they drew blood and then put me in the room to have an ultra sound. The male guard stood watch outside, while the female guard stood right over me during the examination. The doctor was a small-framed Asian female with a no-nonsense type of presence. I was thankful that she did not seem to let my chains inhibit her care. For one moment, I was able to forget my unfortunate set of circumstances and focus on this beautiful new gift of life that was growing at a rapid pace inside of me.

She began to load my belly down with gel, and no sooner than she placed the scanner to my stomach, two heads popped up on the screen. "I got another set of twins over here," she said, "My second one today." I burst into the loudest laugh and cry that I have ever released. I looked at the screen…two babies, twins, I thought. I never imagined having twins. No wonder I was so big. The armed guard standing watch was one of the ones who frequently denied my extra food request. She was a full-figured sister that stood about 6'2", with very full lips that hung in the wind as she stood there, viewing my double blessing.

God had answered my prayers, to give me something so wonderful at that point in my life; I saw it as a sign that I was not alone and that I would be able to make it through this. Even though the answer to my plea came in a truly unexpected manner, I knew that it had come. This would be my ticket home to have my baby… excuse me, babies, knowing that the detention center would not want the responsibility of caring for me in this condition. As soon as we got back to the jail and the Warden heard the good news, I believe they began to work on my bond reduction right away.

I couldn't wait for word to get to Rob. If you think news travels fast on the streets, it travels at the speed of light in the joint. Everybody knows everybody else's business, sometimes even before the individual knows. One of the guards liked us and I was able to get him to give Rob one of the ultra sound pictures. We both began to ponder what we would name them. We had thought about Sojourner if it where a girl, and then we decided to pick a boy's name. We knew that their names must be reflective, in some way, of all that we were going through while working to bring them forth.

One day I got a card from my sister Sandra. She was wishing me well and trying to cheer my spirits up. She offered the name Justice. Rob and I both liked it, so we settled on Justice and Sojourner.

The public defender that had been assigned my case told my mother that they were planning to reduce my bond, but they would not do so until Robert and Ontario had been sentenced and transferred, which was about a week away.

Every evening we went out for recreation for about and hour. Aside from mailing each other letters, this was the only time I got to talk to Robert. He would stand on top of a mattress in his cell and talk to me through the fenced in window while I stood outside. In our efforts to make the best of a bad situation, like Gladys Knight says, at night, I would put my belly in the window and watch him stroke his window pane to signify him caressing my tummy. It wasn't much, but it was all we had.

June 13th came, the date that judgment for our actions would be rendered against Robert and Ontario. Because of our failure to accept the initial plea deal and the jury tampering case, I knew they were gonna throw the book at us, starting with them.

It was late that evening, and I could tell, by the thickness in the atmosphere, that shit around me was brewing. Finally, recreation time came. I could find out how deeply buried into these life choices we were going to be. I posted up in my regular spot outside of Rob's window, and then he appeared. I remember asking him, "How did it go?" But before I could get it out of my mouth good, he replied, "Shit, they gave me sixty years."

IN THE BELLY OF THE BEAST
⚜ Chapter Eight ⚜

Sixty years!

I could not even start to process it. Nobody died. Shit, for that matter, no one even needed medical attention. No prior felonies… and they gave him a life sentence…in a crime in which no life was taken. As I listened to Rob give me the details of the proceedings, I could tell from his suggestions that he had hit an all new low.

I figured that if I could offer him nothing else, I could reassure him that I would stand with him, and told him that no matter what, I would not let go of his hand.

Now don't get me wrong about what I said. I knew that people were harmed from our actions, and I also knew they were gonna come down hard on us. However, I did not figure they would act with such a vengeance and, what I felt was outright an abuse of power, by taking his life, when no one else's was taken.

The only thing we had working in our favor at this point was that with him now sentenced and waiting to be transferred, soon my feet would be back on the ground, and I would be able to work toward some form of relief for our family.

My lawyer met with me shortly after they transferred Robert and Ontario and told me my bond hearing had been set. The judge had agreed to drop my bond from $500,000 to $50,000. I got on the phone and told mama what I would need to get out. She made the phone call, and within a couple of hours after court, I was headed home. Even though it was a small move, considering what we were up against, I did not care if God did not grant another one of my prayers. Right then, I knew I had been removed from experiencing the most inhumane treatment of women in America – I could go home and have my babies and not be forced to deliver life, handcuffed to a bed. Thank the Lord.

When I walked in the house, all I wanted to do was hug my children. From what I had been told, the baby boy, Laurence had been the most traumatized by my absence. I recall his first time visiting me at the jail. Wow! It still makes my eyes fill with tears, just thinking about it. He walked into the visitation area and saw me in prison uniform. He began screaming, "Mama no, no, no, Mama." My mother told me that he had been waking up in the middle of the night, crying out for me, and had even begun wetting the bed. Law (that's what we call him 'cause he tries to keep all of us in line) had been potty-trained before he was two. Now, here he was at three years old, reverting to the baby stage. My actions had inflicted pain on everyone around us.

My time in jail had been my children's longest time ever being without me, and it had truly taken its toll. As for me, I was broke and extremely disappointed by the choices I had made; downtrodden and not really in a position to care for myself. Like Law, I sought the comfort that only a mother's love can give and fell into the arms of my own mother, whose love received me. Did I say, Thank God for mamas?

It was nowhere near over, but I was grateful that I had been granted a brief moment of sweet relief.

The twins were due in November, and being big as I was, employment was not a possibility for me. I felt so helpless, but yet still determined to make it. When Momma closed Culture in the mall, she moved the goods into the space next door to a flea market she owned. It was a small operation, (even the term "mom and pop" was too big to describe the enterprise) but it offered me some form of vitality while I was going through this transition. All I could do was tread water.

There were a couple of things I knew I needed: first, some money, and second, a lawyer to represent me. Robert, communicating by mail from a holding facility north of Shreveport, was trying to encourage me to reopen Culture. But with two small kids and two on the way, I considered it, but did not have the wherewithal needed to get it done. I too, was in a holding place.

Shortly after my birthday, in August, I was approved to visit Robert. Toting a 60-year sentence, and Ontario, a 45-year sentence, they had been sent to what was known as the world's bloodiest prison...Angola State Penitentiary. Initially opened in the 1800's as a breeding plantation and named for the country in Africa that the slaves were imported from, Angola had a long history of serving as a home for blacks, and black men in particular. The prison is still largely a farming plantation, with 18,000 acres and over 5,000 legal slaves to work it. It even has a prison cemetery, for those whose lives will end there and who may not have families that can afford other options. It is the nation's largest maximum security prison.

After a five-hour trip through the swamps and the hills of Louisiana, I reached the front gate. Not having a clue as to what to expect, I was just delighted to know that, for the first time in months, I would be able to sit down and talk with Rob. (He would finally be able to rub my swollen belly.) When two people take as big of a fall together in life as Rob and I had, it will either rip you apart or glue you together.

As time passed, I began to give up hope on having a girl. The latest ultrasound had shown that one of the babies was definitely a boy, but I knew we needed to have a backup boy's name, just in case our hope for a girl didn't pan out. During one of our conversations, Robert reminded me of a guy we knew in Shreveport, whose name was Freedom. He asked me what I thought about the other baby's name being Freedom. Freedom….something we both had gained a tremendous respect for and both desperately desired. Without hesitation, I agreed.

On the anniversary of the Million Man March, October 16, 1999 at 3:16 in the morning, with my mother and my godfather, Frank at my side, I gave birth gave to two healthy baby boys, rightfully named Freedom and Just'us Fox Richardson. I had now mothered four beautiful boys. For a brief moment, I was able to be wrapped up in the bliss that new life brings. However, deep down inside, I knew that with the birth now behind me, the heat would soon be on top of me again.

I needed representation, but I would have to have some money to get it.

Without the love and support of my family, I never would have been able to make it. In December, my oldest sister, Sharon, lost her husband in a terrible accident. Out of the insurance money she received, she loaned me a portion of the money I needed to retain a lawyer.

Empowered with lessons learned from two years of going through the system, I knew what to look for in a lawyer. After doing some extensive research, I found an attorney in Monroe, LaValle Salomon, who did a lot of work in Lincoln Parish. After meeting with him, he agreed to take my case. My next big issue had been solved, thankfully. To go to court with an attorney being paid by the same people prosecuting me would have left me in eminent danger, and very well would have cost me my life.

I know you may be asking, "What are you talking about, Fox Rich?" But think about it. Public defenders are paid by the state. When you are accused of committing a crime, it is the state that prosecutes you (unless you catch a federal charge, then it is the federal government that is bringing charges against you). When you have a public defender, it is the state that also represents you. This is something we all need to be aware of.

It began to settle in on me that I was probably gonna have to do some time, but how much was the question. The uncertainty was like a dark cloud that followed me everywhere I went. I attempted to put some shows together to generate some "going away money," but did not manifest anything substantial. About that time, the phone call came from my lawyer. They were ready for me.

It is said that when the student is ready, the teacher appears. I had heard of a woman by the name of Frankie Muhammad from a close sister friend. While I was awaiting my fate, my cousin Tracey, who was a member of the Nation of Islam, told me about a sister who had done some time, who might be good for me to talk to. It was Sister Frankie. From my first meeting with her, she took me in and shared insight with me that I needed. I would go over to her house a few times a week and she would meditate and pray with me. We would burn frankincense and sage, and light a candle.

Even though Sister Frankie would "let you have it," she was a prayer warrior. From there, I believe I was able to connect to my Higher Power, to gain the strength that would later be required of me. Sister Frankie made her transition from this life in September of 2007, but the love she shared with me in my time of need lives on in my spirit.

It was June 2000, and I was to report to court for my pretrial conference. I had been coming on a monthly basis from the time I had been released from the doctor's care, but it was always the usual continuances to the next month. But now however, their attention had turned back to me, and boy, were they ready for me.

We were in our third year of dealing with this situation, and it was my turn at bat. After the scheduled proceedings, my lawyer met with me and broke the news, "You are looking at 12 years, without the possibility of parole." He went on to explain the process. I was eligible to receive "good time," meaning I would only serve half my time, with good behavior. "Worst case scenario," he said, "You are looking at having to serve six years." Six years: he said it like it was nothing, but it seemed like an eternity to me.

It brings tears to my eyes just thinking about it. I was 28, and after 6 years I would be almost 35. "That's a lot of time," I said. He replied, "Well it is a far cry from their first offer of 40 years, then they went down to 20. "Right now," he said, "I got them down to 12 years, worst case scenario." But he committed to keep working on them before the next scheduled court date in July. In the meantime, he wanted me to get my mind prepared and my affairs in order.

I had been home on bond for a year, and the time had finally come when I would have to pay the piper. These days, judges are giving out time like candy, which is one of the reasons Louisiana has more of its citizens locked up per capita than any other place on the planet... unless, of course, you believe we lead the world in incarceration because all the bad people live here. They claim to be doing this to be "tough on crime," a mind-set that has done nothing to decrease or deter crime in our state. This is obvious, because our state still has two cities on the top ten list of the nation's most dangerous cities and leads the country in gun-related deaths per capita.

I met with my biggest supporter in all of this mess, my mother, and told her what I was facing. In her calm and collected voice she replied, "Sibil, go on, do what you gotta do and get that behind you. Me and these boys will be alright." (Every time I think of that conversation, tears run from my eyes.) I had not even begun to process the fact that I was about to have to leave all four of my children behind, and who would be responsible for their welfare. I was still busy just trying to get past the fact that I was about to go serve some time. However, my mother was thinking ahead and had already prepared herself to assume responsibility for my boys. Again, did I say how thankful I am for family and my mother's love? Unlike most people who go to prison, I was blessed with time to get my personal affairs in order.

Out of sheer disappointment and disgust with myself, I turned to my godfather Frank for wise counsel. I liked talking my concerns over with Frank because he had a way of putting it plain and simple, but without judgment and ridicule. He listened attentively, as I rambled on about my failures and how my life had come to nothing. I shared how I was well on my way to a good life; had completed my masters degree, purchased my first home at 25, began teaching college, and opened my first business. Now, I was done, reduced to nothing, and in my mind, would be an old ass woman by the time I made it out of the joint.

Frank stood there, and looked at me like I was talking out the side of my neck, when he asked me, "Sibil, if you come into this life and do everything you are supposed to do by the time you are 25, what the hell you need the other 60 or 70 years for? Life is a process." If that was not rocket science made simple, like first grade math. Even greater, it was reassurance for me that my life was not over. After I got this behind me, I could begin working on the next season of my life. Frank was a blessed inspiration during my time of darkness. His words helped me to think straight and enabled me to see light at the end of the tunnel.

The next person I would have to talk with was my biggest fan... Remington. I decided that I would get a good night's rest, (as good as you can get when you find out you're about to do some time), then I would take him for a walk the next morning in our favorite park. There, I could talk to him, one-on-one. I knew that with four children, and two of them only 10 months old, my mother would rely heavily on Remi , who was soon-to-be seven years old. But because I believe he is an old man locked in a young man's body, I knew he would handle it.

Aside from the experience of going to my first ob/gyn appointment in handcuffs and shackles, telling Remi I was about to leave him was the most heartbreaking. I shot it to him as straight as I could, probably one of the reasons to this day that we are so close. I've never held anything back from him. The good, the bad, and the ugly, I have openly, though sometimes grudgingly, shared.

As planned, that next morning we headed out, just he and I. After engaging in some small talk we stopped on the trail and I bent down to his eye level and said, "Baby, I know I told you I would be here, and I have done everything I can to stay here with you, but unfortunately, the people in charge feel like I need to do some time for what I did."

There had been many moments before that I genuinely regretted what we had done. But no moment felt as bad as when I had to tell my six-year old baby, (who I even took to college with me, rather than leave him), that because of choices his father and I had made, I was going to have to leave him for up to six years, and that I needed him to stand in as man of the house.

I held him, and we both cried uncontrollably. When we had gotten it out of our system, his next question was how long I would be gone. I told him that if they didn't change their minds, worst case scenario, he would be 13 by the time I got home. He cried again. At age 6, I am sure that 13 seemed light years away.

By the time we finished our walk, I had talked to him about how his grandmother would need his help. He committed to holding the family down for me. I further instructed him that we would now start our countdown to my departure date and try to make the most of the time we would have left together. He happily agreed, only after I told him that I was happy about counting down my departure, because the sooner I left, the sooner I could get back to him and get this behind us. He hugged me and told me he loved me.

Even at my lowest moment, he still loved me unconditionally. God is good.

The next phase of my mission was to secure support for the boys who were about to start school. On the first day of school, I met with Laurence's teacher. He was just starting kindergarten. Remington was going into the second grade. I met with their respective principals to inform them of my upcoming departure, so they could know that my children have special needs. Both their parents would be absent. That little bit of preparation helped make a big difference. To this day, Remington's second grade teacher, Mrs. Mayeaux, is still one of his favorites.

Other help came in the form of friends and family members that committed to assist my mother in my absence. For instance, Remington's god-mother, Tulip Frazier, has done an amazon job throughout the years. So much so that if you looked up the word "god-mother" in the dictionary, her picture would be featured next to the definition of the word. Coach Balwin and his family made it a point to carry the boys to the Louisiana Tech football games. I had sister friends, like Lillian Priest and Janie Samuel, who would drop off school clothes for the boys, and pick them up and take them to the movies. Roxanne Johnson bought the double stroller needed for the twins. My sister, Sandra, kept all of them over the summer and my brother, Sredni, and his wife took all four of them every weekend. The list just goes on and on, of the random acts of kindness that came our way. We were very fortunate to receive a whole lot of love, while we walked through hell.

On August 31, 2000, I awoke at 4:00 am, and began to prepare to go and serve my time. I drove downtown to the riverfront and sat in solitude as I looked over the city, I prayed and said to myself, "If they're gonna give me some time out, I promise, I'm gonna put it to good use." I smoked me one and sat there in contemplation of what was to come. As I returned home to do what I had to do - the pain was heart-wrenching – the pity party set in. Look what I had done to my life and those I loved.

I woke my oldest boys and kissed them good-bye. Then I saw my mother off to the hospital with Freedom. He had been born with two fully-formed extra fingers and was scheduled to have surgery to remove them that same morning. I could feel the deeply-rooted disappointment and hurt in my mother as I attempted to say farewell.

Escorted by my godfather, I reported to Lincoln Parish courthouse, and there was remanded into the custody of the state of Louisiana, to serve one five-year sentence and two seven-year sentences, to be run concurrently (If you don't know what that means, 'cause I didn't before I got in this shit, it means at the same time). My attorney told me he would work on my time and he did. Instead of serving 6 years, I would be home in 3½. Did I say God is good?

A SLAVE AGAIN
 Chapter Nine

How do a free people check themselves back into slavery? I've got my own opinions, but regardless the reason; it's still a damn shame. Here our people have worked for centuries to be free, and with the power invested in me, I had turned myself into a slave, again.

I was held for about two weeks at the Lincoln Parish Detention Center. This time was different from the last time I was there. At least I had an exit date out of this system. Now, for the first time in years, I knew that my part of this was coming to an end.

One of the guards drove me to Rayville, Louisiana, to the Richland Parish Detention Center, where I would be serving my sentence. I could go on and on, talking about how these small parishes are getting monies for their towns by taking advantage of our overcrowded state prison system. I could talk at length about how people are being warehoused, for extended periods of time, in places that offer no programs to help them improve themselves before their release dates. Without programs available to rehabilitate inmates, taxpayers will keep footing the bill for their next trip back to jail. But that ain't this book. That one will come later.

When I got there, I was on a mission. I wanted to speak. I wanted to empower others and lift them up. I remembered the advice from Adele Givens. I thought to myself, what better place to start honing my craft than right where I was, walking among some of the most down-trodden sisters in society? I did not want to waste any time, so my first week there, one night, I stood up on my bunk in a dormitory room filled with 75 women, and said, "May I have your attention, please?" And they gave it to me. Amazing what you can get, when you ask for it. That night my message was entitled "Humpty Dumpty." I know you think it's elementary, but my goal was to remind them that no matter what situation we were in, we could put our lives back together.

I've been speaking ever since. When you love doing something, you don't wait until the conditions are right to do it; you do it and the conditions will follow.

I had been there seven months when the rumor spread that I was writing a book. (This book has been a long time coming. I started working on it when I first went to prison, ten years ago). The Warden decided to ship me to another facility in Rapides Parish, in Alexandria, Louisiana. I was there for a week, and then landed in Cotton Port, Louisiana, at Avollyes Parish Detention Center. That is where I met Mr. Johnson, the GED instructor who helped me get to the women's prison, so that I could apply for the boot camp program.

Robert had been doing some research, and had told me about a program called boot camp, or intensive incarceration, for non-violent offenders. It was a program that even if the judge had not sentenced me to, I could apply directly. What it meant was that after six months of training, I could be back at home with my boys and spend the rest of my time under intensive parole supervision. This did not bother me because I knew that I would never do anything that would put me at risk of them getting me like that again. (They will never get me like that again.)

I went on the interview for the program, only to be turned down;

to this day I am unclear why. However, I had a backup plan. If I did not get in, at least I knew that I could go to work release from there. As a non-violent offender, you can go to work release with up to a year left to serve. Detention centers, unlike state prisons, don't want to let go of their paychecks (the state inmates) until they have to. Seldom would they allow their prisoners to leave for work release, unless they were court ordered. On the other hand, state facilities had training programs that you could take to gain skills. Once space was available, eligible inmates could go to work release. I started off working in the kitchen and then enrolled in a computer course offered through vo-tech. Through this course, I was able to improve myself and enhance my employability beyond the college degrees I had already attained.

Another great thing offered at the women's prison was the Angel Tree program, which granted me a little of my humanity while I was away. During Christmas, the Angel Tree program would set aside a bag of gifts for each child of an inmate scheduled to come to the Christmas celebration they put on. We even got a chance to wrap the gifts our children would receive. I can't tell you what it did for me to be able to celebrate Christmas with my boys and then give them gifts from me from behind bars. They were so happy. To all the Angel Tree workers out there, please keep up the good work. You cannot even begin to measure the difference you are making in the lives of others.

After I graduated from the computer program, I was eligible for work release and was shipped to a halfway house in Lake Charles. There I got a job cleaning hotel rooms. I thought that I would be able to find my own job, once at the halfway house, only to discover that you could only work at the places the program had contracts with.

Then I found out that one of the girls worked as a manger at Burger King, so I had my eye on a new hustle. I was thinking that Burger King would have a computer I could use. However, transferring jobs would require a great deal of politicking. The lady who ran the house was one of the meanest I had met. She was not concerned at all with helping those she served. She didn't want me to change jobs, even though the open position of shift manager at Burger King meant a pay raise. So, I went over her head.

The new gig at Burger King was just what I was hoping for – computer access, so I could start writing again. And as the universe would have it, one day the owner of the local black publication, *Gumbeaux Magazine*, came in. After talking with me at length, he agreed to print my work. I would arrive an hour before my shift every morning to write my articles to be published.

After just a few months of writing that weekly newspaper article, I found myself being snatched off my job and *shipped*. Normally when you got shipped, it was because you had done something wrong. I was taken back to the facility and instructed to pack my bags. I was going to a halfway house in Monroe, the City of Faith. This was very unusual, because it was understood that inmates could not be transferred between halfway houses. When I got to the City of Faith, I found out that someone had called in a favor to have me relocated. The power of the pen will definitely get things moving.

That is when things really began to look up, because at the halfway house in Monroe, they allowed you to attend college and find your own job. Because my dream for our next business venture was a TV show, I figured I could enroll in the master's program in mass communication at the local college and get to work.

I got a full scholarship, a graduate assistantship, and a student loan. Who said school doesn't pay? I also got a job working for the public relations director for one of the largest nonprofits in the Monroe area, Booker T. Community Outreach. I am not saying large because of the size of the organization, but I am speaking of the spirit of its founder Esther Gallot, a full-sized, no-holds-barred woman, who was a true mover and shaker in the Monroe area, whose reputation preceded her. You want something done? Give it to Esther. I admired her so greatly that I adopted her as my Godmother.

I assisted and watched in awe as she built a 3.5 million dollar assisted living facility to serve low-income seniors who do not need or want to go to a nursing home. It was rightfully named after one of the former senators who supported the project from the beginning; the John Breaux Assisted Living Facility.

Another great thing about this halfway house was that as long as you were making legal money, you could work anywhere. The other job I took on was speaking. I got my first paid speaking engagement delivering a keynote address for the Louisiana Black Mayors' Association Conference that August. Then the historic Mount Zion Baptist Church opened its doors to me. Next, was the big Arcadia back-to-school rally, sponsored by Pastor Wortham and his church. Others followed. That is when things really began to change for me.

Often, I would speak, and someone would hear my first name, Sibil and mistake me for Sybil on the Tom Joyner Show, a tremendous compliment, but pretty disappointing when you have to tell people you are not who they think you are. Sometimes I would not even have the heart to tell them.

At this event two significant things happened: first, the juror who reported us to the Sheriff was first cousin to the pastor that booked me to speak, and she had come to share with me. I know, deep, huh? Then, after the presentation, a little girl came up to me with her mother, crying, "Oh, Ms. Sybil, I love you so much! I listen to you everyday." That was it for me. I knew that Tom Joyner's Sybil had my first name sewed up, and if I was ever gonna build a name for myself, I needed to find another one.

When I got back to the dorm, and was working on the cover for my first motivational CD, it dawned on me to just discontinue the use of my first name and use my last two; Fox and Rich. Now, I bet you haven't heard of one of those. I would no longer be embarrassed by someone thinking I was someone I was not. It had come to be pretty humiliating, but now I had a solution. And a good one at that.

I spent the last eleven months of my sentence on work release and was able to position myself for a strong return home.

PHOTOS & DOCUMENTS
⚜ Chapter Ten ⚜

Photo A: Rob and me getting married

Photo B:
Friends we met during the honeymoon

Photo C: bottom: Owners of LA Signs, Robert and me.

Photo D:
Putting the finishing touches on the outside of "Cullture"

Photo E: The front of "Culture"

Photo F: Rob and me with Tito (left)

Photo G: Rob and me with Naughty By Nature

Photo H: Young supporters of the store

Photo I: Culture store manager, Aiesha and me, holding it down.

Photo K: Yes, we even had the floor of "Culture" tricked out.

Photo L: Culture in the mall

Photo J: Rob and me inside a fully-stocked Culture;

Photo N: left to right:
Nephew Tommy, Rob, Jabba Jaws, and „Bra Man from Martin

Photo O: Me with Adele Givens at a Culture Party

WARRANT

STATE OF LOUISIANA

versus

SIBIL V. FOX

STATE OF LOUISIANA

PARISH OF LINCOLN

To the Sheriff of the Parish of Lincoln:—Greeting—

Whereas, ____TONY OSBON, INVESTIGATOR FOR THE DISTRICT ATTORNEY____ has this day made complaint, under oath, before me, Judge of the District Court, Parish of Lincoln, that on or about the ____15th____ day of ____September____, 19_97_, one ____Sibil V. Fox____ _____at and in said Parish

did commit the offense of armed robbery on the Grambling Credit Union in violation of R.S. 14:64.

These are therefore to Command You, in the name of the State of Louisiana, to forthwith arrest the said ____SIBIL V. FOX____, and take him before the District Judge of the Parish of Lincoln, to answer unto said complaint, and to be further dealt with according to law.

Herein fail not, and due return make of this writ.

Given under my hand officially, at my office in Ruston, in said Parish and State, this____17th____ day of ____September____ A.D., 19 _97_ .

Cynthia J. Woodard

Judge/Justice of the Peace

Photo P: My Arrest Warrant

66

C23610

LINCOLN PARISH
DETENTION CENTER
RUSTON, LOUISIANA

JAIL CARD # _____

Date Arrested _Sept. 26_____ 19_97_   Time _11:10_   A.M. / P.M.

Name _Sibil Verdette Fox_ AKA _Richardson_   ID # _____

Address _3321 Linda St. Shreveport, La. 71119_   DOB _08-18-71_

Race _B_   Sex _F._   Age _26_   Height _5'2"_   Weight _155_

Charge _Armed Robbery_ w/t. 97-005846

Place Arrested _LPDC_

Amount of Bond _$50,000.00_

Bondsman _Judy Waddard_

Date Released _Sept. 26_____ 19_97_   Time _12:25_   A.M. / P.M.

Date to Appear _Oct. 31, 1997- (9:00 A.M.)_

Drivers License # _____   STATE ____ TYPE ____ EXP. ____

Social Security # _____

Occupation _Self employed_

Remarks EYE- BRN.   STATUS- _Pre Trial_

HAIR- BLK.   CO-DEFENDANT- _Ontario Smith / Robert Richardson_

P.O.B.- Houston, Tex.   PHONE _318·636·6818_

Disposition _____

Capt. C. Smith
BOOKING OFFICER
Signature

I Den
ARRESTING OFFICER
Signature

Louisiana Correctional Institute
For Women

Name Sybil Fox
DOC# 387410
Race Black

LCIW INMATE

Photo Q: My Jail Card and I.D

Photo R: Fox Rich Show Ticket

Photo S: Hyping the Fox Rich TV show.

Photo T: Working on the set of the Fox Rich Show

Photo M: Lobby of Fox Rich Studios

Photo U: Collage of some of the talent and audiences from the Fox Rich Show

Photo V: Promo for first CD

Photo W: Eryka Badu performs on the Fox Rich Show

Photo X: The family visit at Angola Penitentiary

Photo Y:
The Twins,
Freedom and Justus Richardson

Photo Z:
Close up of Robert Richardson

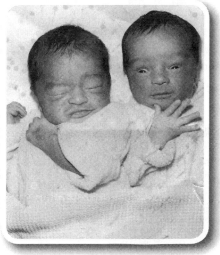

THE RISE OF FOX RICH
⚜ Chapter Eleven ⚜

With my educational credits and my good time, I was released from the halfway house on October 23, my mother's birthday; a great present for a grandmother taking care of four boys. And you can imagine the very first thing I did...I went and got my Rich brothers. All four of those little spirits had been on this horrible journey with me, and I knew they longed for me just as much as I had been yearning for them.

The first mission was to connect with them and then to show my mother a token of my appreciation. Many of the incarcerated women I met reminded me of how blessed I was, having as many children as I did, to have one person willing to take care of all of them. I found that other female prisoners either had their children separated and living in multiple homes, or they landed in the state's custody and they would have to get home and then fight for their custody to be restored.

As a show of gratitude, I bought her and one of her sisters a plane ticket to D.C. to visit my sister, Sandra, who lived there. Unfortunately, my aunt refused to fly, (it was after Sept 11, and they were still looking for the DC sniper), so my cousin Tracey went in her place.

My next stop was to see the man I had been writing to for the past few years, who had given me the encouragement and inspiration I so desperately needed to get through it all...my husband and fall partner, Robert Richardson.

I made plans with the boys to head to Angola at what had been our usual time of 3:00 am. In order to visit all day we needed to be at the penitentiary by 8:00 am. It takes about five hours to get to Angola from Shreveport, so visitation is a journey within itself.

I can't recall many of the details of that first visit, just a slight feeling of relief...I did not have "the people" after me, so that gave me some small peace of mind. But my mind was still cloudy, as I tried to adjust to my new freedom.

You truly don't know what freedom means until you have been a slave. The interesting thing I discovered is that you don't have to be locked behind prison walls to be a prisoner. In this life, there are many things, people and situations that will lock us up and have us so discombobulated that, in a state of confusion, we don't even realize that we have the keys to set ourselves free.

We spent a few days bonding with Robert and trying to reaffirm, revitalize and renew our family ties, which we had all suffered the loss of. The boys had not seen or spoken with their father since I had left, and our contact had been minimized to letters. The visit was our own small family reunion.

After visitation days where over, I knew it was time for me to get to work. There were a lot of people counting on me...and many others waiting on me to fail.

Before my release, I began setting in motion plans to create a television program. After watching a weekly program called "The Ernie Myles Show" that aired in the detention center, I decided there was a great need for programming where people could showcase their talents. Robert and I discussed, at length, the feasibility of such an undertaking, and in our spirits knew it would work.

Even with two college degrees, I knew that coming out of prison with a felony record would make finding viable employment like trying to find a needle in a haystack. I knew for certain that my best bet was to create employment for myself. A TV show would give me a job and also allow me to do what I loved.

My initial thinking was that I would get home, and in maybe six months to a year I would launch the program. However, Robert thought it could be done a lot sooner, and shared his vision with me on how we could get it done.

I moved home in January, and with my student loan money and some help from a family friend, I began to put things in motion. We decided to return to South Park Mall, the location of our last business, Culture Clothing Store, and leased what had been a small, two-cinema movie studio. The mall was delighted to have us, since there had been a decrease in tenants. He believed that this concept would draw traffic, and let us rent the site for utilities only. Rightfully so, because the studio needed so much work, it wasn't even funny. It was a project within itself.

All of the seats and the interior needed painting, and without a budget, it meant I would have to do it myself. Over the course of about two weeks, the show dancers, my nephew Adriel, and my nine-year-old son Remington removed 320 seat bottoms and tops, cleaned them, painted them, and replaced them. We had the studio ready to go by the end of January.

The demand for the product that I was presenting was so great that even on a national scale the concept was being implemented. A few months before our debut, the television show called American

Idol began airing. I knew we were on course.

The next major undertaking was the airtime. The best deal I found was with the Fox Network. I brokered a contract with them and began my search for talent.

Only four months after getting out of prison, we started, with no budget and a small staff of volunteers, like my cousin Avery Mathews, and Robert "Bubba" Birmingham, the father of one of my dancers. Their creative minds helped me design a set, using scraps and leftover materials, which looked like it was straight out of Hollywood. Bubba's wife served as the makeup artist, and interns like Carteya, Ashley, and Jerrod helped by assisting me in coordinating the tapings and auditions for the show, as well as marketing and promoting it. Their help was priceless.

On March 16, 2003, the Fox Rich Show began airing. In retrospect, I am still amazed at the people who graced our stage. With talent like Eryka Badu, Hurricane Chris, Nayrock, and the R&B group, Profyle, we gave the community a great lineup. Much of the amateur talent was very good...and Lord knows, we had some that were not so good...but even they were good for a hearty laugh.

With no budget, after only two months on air, we pulled in a 3 in the Nielsen ratings May Sweep. This, according to the station's general manager was totally unheard of for paid programming. It showed that not only were we on, but people were definitely watching.

We ran the show for a year. Then we decided it was time to hit the road to pursue my desire for empowering folks who, like me, had hit rock bottom and were trying to find their way back. I started on a mission to share with people my story and the obstacles I had overcome, so that they can use it as fuel to overcome obstacles in their own lives.

In January of 2005 I launched the Fox Rich Power Party Tour, a motivational lecture series that travels across the nation to colleges and universities, empowering and uplifting our people. To this day, the tour continues to reach out to the masses, uplifting the human spirit. Did I say God has been good?

Henry David Thoreau said, "Regardless of what lies behind us or what lies ahead of us, nothing is more powerful than that which lies within us."

A PRISONER'S WIFE
❧ Chapter Twelve ❧

In May of 2006 I completed my parole. A few months later I gave birth to what would be *our* sixth son, Robert Fox Richardson. It was during this time that I found the need for medical benefits. Being self-employed has its benefits, but the cost of medical insurance is not one of them. It was this experience that has caused me to support my president and his call for universal health care. It also led me to seek employment that offered benefits.

In 2007, I found a place in the job market that would look beyond my past transgressions and give me an opportunity to be a contribution to their organization...I began selling high line cars with a focus on Cadillacs. Not only do I sell Cadillacs, but at this writing I am the lead salesperson at my dealership. Not bad, for the only woman in an all-male workplace. The additional income has enhanced my family's quality of life and allowed me to meet some very interesting folks. Not everybody can own a Cadillac, so it has been nice to mingle everyday with those who can.

On the family front, Robert had been gone 12 years when I came to a decision to dissolve our marriage. When two people are joined in holy matrimony, but yet are not living as husband and wife, it places an immeasurable strain on the union, especially when you throw in the inhumane conditions that incarceration can wreak on a family.

While Louisiana leads the world in incarceration per capita, it does little toward reinforcing family ties. There are many states in the union that allow conjugal visits. When you are incarcerated, you not only lose your freedom, you seemingly lose your humanity as well.

I say that because a person is denied the very thing I think makes us HUMAN BE-INGS...humanly contact. Next to your will to live, scientist say, your strongest drive is your sex drive. Restricting conjugal visits, in my opinion, not only diminishes one's humanity, it also promotes homosexuality inside the institution, but that's another story for another day.

Over the course of his absence I became financially, emotionally, and spiritually depleted, and realized if I were going to survive, I would have to release myself from our union. It was one of the hardest decisions I have made in my life, yet I felt, a necessary one. Robert and I are continuing to work toward our family's restoration. We know that his freedom is key, if we plan to put our marriage back together. Our situation, in so many ways, resembles slavery to me. I think back often, to how it must have been to maintain a union with someone, when that man or woman belonged to someone else. In the past it was the plantation master. In our present case, my life's partner's master is the State of Louisiana.

Maintaining the institution of marriage under normal circumstances is hard, but when you add slavery, it takes on a whole new level of difficulty...but not impossibility. I would ask you to keep us in your prayers, as we continue to attempt to repair what we broke. When I married Robert, I did so because I wanted what I did not have growing up: the "nuclear family", where my mother and father lived under the same roof.

Now, with the separation, I realize that the most valuable thing we ever had or could have had was not in that bank; it was in us and the power that one has when you have family.

HIGHER CALLING
 Chapter Thirteen

My desire to share our struggle is not about just us, but about the millions of American families, in particular black families, that are out there going through the same things we have been through, and yet continue to endure...' cause it ain't over yet.

During our time of separation, Robert created an organization to work toward making a difference in our community by keeping our people out of the system.

LRND, the acronym for Living Responsibly Never Deviating, has a mission to: 1) decrease the number of our people that enter the criminal justice system; 2) work to release those who have been unjustly imprisoned or excessively sentenced; 3) break this vicious cycle of incarceration that is plaguing our community; 4) work with children who are orphaned, as a result of incarceration, and address their special needs.

I have served on the Governor's Board for Juvenile Justice and Delinquency Prevention for six years, under two administrations. One of the main statistics that has stuck out in my mind is that 85 % of all juveniles doing time have a parent locked up. So, if we want to change those numbers and turn this thing around, the best thing we can do is begin working with those children, orphaned by virtue of incarceration.

One of the major lessons I gained from the Jena Six and my own plight is, that once you get in the system there is no guarantee that we can get you out. So the best thing we can do for ourselves as well as for those we love is, keep our ass (by any means necessary) out of the system's web.

Robert and I have many regrets, but we both believe that if we can just save one life from choosing this path, we have done a mighty work. What we had to learn the hard way is all worth it if we can help someone else choose better for themselves.

I heard our president make a national call for us all to do something to make America better. Robert, serving as the founder of LRND, and I, working as its coordinator, are on a mission to do just that.

I said it before but must say it again; when our loved ones pay their debts to society we all pay. We pay when we have to take from the family's resources to bond them out. We pay when we have to hire a lawyer for them; we pay when we have to get off work to go back and forth to court with them; we pay when we have to put money on their books; we pay when we have to accept their collect calls; we pay when we have to visit them; we pay when we suffer the loss that their absence in our community brings; we pay, we pay, we pay and we continue to pay, when they return home and can't find employment due to their record, or can't vote because of their felony status.

When you get a felony on your record you and your family will pay your debt to society for the rest of your natural born life. Again I say; if you get nothing else from this book, get this: WE MUST STAY CLEAR OF THEIR SYSTEM.

I was listening to the Tom Joyner Show, when Jeff Johnson came on with his commentary. It was shortly after we had launched LRND. He talked about the power of the AARP organization and how strong they are because of their numbers. Then he went on to compare their numbers to the number of offenders and ex-offenders in this country. He suggested that a strong organization could be built if these people came together collectively to address the system and its quirks.

Robert and I are working to make LRND that voice for offenders, ex-offenders, and their families. I know we are all hurting from the same pain. Therefore, I would like to invite you to join us in our efforts. Become a member of an organization built for the sole purpose of breaking the cycle of incarceration which is plaguing our community. Together we can place our focus on prevention and not detention.

There is not one black person who doesn't know someone in their family who is or has been locked up. It is time to unify our efforts and redirect the course of our people bound for the system.

To become a part of this movement, visit our website at www.LRND.org.

WHAT I'VE LRND

⚜ Chapter Fourteen ⚜

I have learned so much, and still I am learning so much more. This experience transformed me and made me realize what the really important things are in life.

I have learned that when you've got life, you've got everything you need to make it. I have often heard how the present is a gift, and I now understand why. As long as you have life, you have another chance to transform yourself from who you are to who you want to become; to move from where you are to where you want to be. When I went to prison, I lost all of the things that I thought were important, only to discover that as long as I had breath in my body, my health and my strength, I could continue to, as the Bible says, "...do all things through Christ Jesus that strengthens me."

That Divine Intelligence that makes our heart continue to beat, our lungs expand and deflate, our ears hear and eyes see and food digest, without any direction from us at all, lets us know that, no matter what state we are in, God is always within us, for God is us. As long as we live, life will always be our greatest fortune, for it is through life that everything else is possible.

I now know that money is not man's most valuable asset. Love is. When you've got love, you've got something that sets you apart from the masses. When you have love, you have everything you need to make it. Love is the most divine chemical in the universe and it dissolves everything that is not of itself. To be loved unconditionally means that whether you are up or down, rich or poor, sick or well, you have someone who does not just love you for who you are, but they even love you for what you one day might become. It's something we can all use more of.

While at the women's prison, I received a newsletter from Iyanla Vanzant's ministry. The headline article read, "I stopped looking for love everywhere I went and started taking it with me." I suggest that we all become the reflection of love that we would like to see in the world.

More often than not, the first place we are introduced to a concept of love is in our families. That's another of my great lessons learned; ain't nothing more important than your family. Family is as essential to us as human beings as oxygen. We see so many people rejecting an opportunity to build a family, and instead, settling for individualism.

The institution of family is the strongest institution known to mankind. Family is such a strong entity, that you can see a respect for it, even in the animal kingdom, when you look at the lions that travel in prides, or the wolves that travel in packs, or even the fish that travel in schools. The animal kingdom knows the power in numbers and the importance of sticking together. Now does that mean that they will not fight among themselves? No. But above all, they know that they are stronger together than apart.

You ain't feeling me, so let me take it a step further, to the insect kingdom. Anytime you see an ant, you know for sure that there is not just one ant, because if you see one there are plenty more somewhere around. Okay, let's go on and take it down home. If you look around your house and see a roach, you know damn well you don't just have one roach. You've got roaches, 'cause they comin' in droves.

We need each other. Let me say it again: We Need Each Other to be stronger, wiser, better human beings. Lonely is the man who walks this life alone, for he is missing the power found in a clan. Family doesn't just include people that you share the same bloodline with, but can also include important relationships that you have formed with those around you.

Another crucial lesson that I must share, drawn from this experience, is that the universal laws do not change. You can dress them up in any religion you choose, but they remain the same. You will reap what you sow. If you want good things to follow you all the days of your life, go around doing good. If you want a blessing, become a blessing for someone else. You only get back what you send out. Many of us don't have much good happening in our lives because we spend a majority of our time up to no good.

Don't block your blessings. Do not get distracted and stop giving or helping because you helped someone and they did not even say "Thank you." People cannot give you what they don't have. But trust and know that when you perform a good work, it will come back, although it may not come back through the individual for which it was done.

Lastly, we only have this life, make it count! All of us on this planet have been given something great...LIFE. What we do with it is totally up to us. We can blame other people, situations and circumstances for our lack of success, but at the end of the day, our life is totally our responsibility. Therefore, we must be gentle with it, and treat it with care.

I was leaving the funeral services for the mother of two of my Sunday School students at Little Union Baptist Church, when I overheard a couple of gentlemen outside; talking about the last time they had seen the deceased. They went on and on about how they just could not believe she was gone. The thought passed through my mind as I walked away, "Where do we get this from? Acting like we're always supposed to be here...ain't nobody promised us no tomorrow." We cannot get out of this life alive.

I said that to say, live life to the fullest while you are here. Some people live a short amount of time and leave such an impact on the world, that their names go down in history. Hundreds of years later, those who walk the earth are still saying their names. Then, some people live such unproductive lives, that shortly after they are gone, their mark is erased.

While an inmate at St. Gabriel, I belonged to the Toastmasters' organization. At one of our meetings, we had to deliver a seven-minute speech about a person who changed the world. One of the lifers in our organization stood up to deliver her message. She stated her title, "39 years: Too long, too short or just long enough?" She went on to share the life of Dr. Martin Luther King Jr. and all the great works he accomplished in his lifetime. Then she said, "It's not about how much time you get here, as much as it is how wisely you use the time you have been given."

Since I was a little girl, I've heard my mama not only tell me, "Sibil you can make it if you try," I watched her do it. These are the same words that I held on to, even as I watched my life flash before me. "Yes, I can. Yes, I can. Yes, I can make it through this," I told myself over and over again, until I began to believe it.

At this point in my life, I know that we are only separated by what we believe. All of our actions or lack thereof are based on our beliefs.

To quote the best selling book in the history of mankind, "faith the size of a mustard seed can move a mountain." When you believe in something, you literally give it power.

I had reached the pit of hell in my life. I had reached the point of no return. But because I was crazy enough or bold enough to take hold of God's word, I made it back. God is still in the miracle business.

No matter where you are on your life's path, please know that you can make it if you try. You can give up on a lot of stuff in your lifetime; a diet plan, a relationship a job...but whatever you do, don't you ever give up on yourself -- you are all you've got.

We will not always make the best decisions; however, as long as we wake in the morning, God gives us a chance to fix it. If God can forgive us for our shortcomings then certainly we should be able to forgive ourselves. Don't let the bad choices of your past immobilize you. And look past those who try to keep you locked into your yesterday.

Find the beauty in your life even when it is wrapped up in hardship and turmoil. When we can begin to find life's beauty, in spite of our circumstances, then we are empowered with the ability to see the light at the end of the tunnel. Just like the storms that come along as we are traveling on the highway, if you can manage to just keep on going, no matter how bad the weather, no matter how long the road, brighter days are just ahead. Just keep on keeping on.

Finally, I must remind you to never, ever, give up on your dreams. No one knows what you have come into this life to do, so don't let others dissuade you with their thoughts of what is possible for you. Hold on to your dreams for dear life, for one day they will become your reality, if you are willing to believe.

If you need an example, please allow my story to serve as proof that anything is possible for you...if you believe.

I believe.

I believe in you.

I believe in me, and I believe in the power that is we. Promise me that you, too, will believe...With God all things are possible. Now go ahead, create the life you desire for yourself.

These are the lessons I've LRND.

FOX RICH

AUGUST 31, 2009

JUST WHO IS FOX RICH?

- a Shreveport native and mother of five, who has experienced the highs and lows of life

- a graduate of Grambling State University who earned a master's degree in Public Administration

- an entrepreneur who started one of the first Hip-Hop clothing shops in the Southern United States

- current host of the Fox Rich Radio Show and former host of the Fox Rich Television Show

- a former inmate who faced a 297 year sentence

- a member of the Louisiana Governor's Board for Juvenile and Delinquency Prevention for the past six years

- currently the lead salesperson at a dealership for high-line luxury vehicles

- the coordinator for LRND (pronounced learned), Living Responsibly Never Deviating, a membership organization dedicated to ending the cycle of incarceration. LRND was founded by Robert Richardson, Fox's life partner and the father of her children.

To schedule speaking engagements or guest appearances for Fox Rich contact her by e-mail at foxrich@foxrich.com or call 866.701.9594

For more information visit the website at www.LRND.org.
